A FEW GOOD HABITS

The Uncomplicated Path to Less Stress and More Success

A FEW GOOD HABITS

The Uncomplicated Path to Less Stress and More Success

JULIE LOWE

Dog-Eared Prose & Press

A Few Good Habits: The Uncomplicated Path
to Less Stress and More Success

ISBN 979-8-9882551-0-9
Library of Congress Control Number: 2023911796
Printed in the United States of America by Dog-Eared Prose & Press
For permissions requests, speaking inquiries, and bulk-order purchase
options, email support@sociallyaligned.com.

Publisher's Cataloging-in-Publication Data
Names: Lowe, Julie, 1977- .
Title: A few good habits : the uncomplicated path to less stress and more
    success / Julie Lowe.
Description: [United States] : Dog-Eared Prose & Press, 2023. | Summary:
    Provides actionable advice for reducing stress and improving daily life
    by challenging traditional personal development myths and focusing
    on four impactful habits.
Identifiers: LCCN 2023911796 | ISBN 9798988255109 (pbk.)
Subjects: LCSH: Habit. | Stress management. | Success. | Mind and body.
    | BISAC: SELF-HELP / Self-Management / Stress Management. |
    SELF-HELP / Personal Growth / Success. | SELF-HELP / Personal
    Growth / General.
Classification: LCC BF335.L69 2023 | DDC 152.33 L--dc23
LC record available at https://lccn.loc.gov/2023911796

This is a work of nonfiction. Nonetheless, the names, personal characteristics of individuals, and details of events have been changed to disguise identities or protect the privacy of the author's clients. Any resulting resemblance to persons living or dead is entirely coincidental and unintentional. The author of this book does not dispense medical advice or prescribe the use of any technique, either directly or indirectly, as a form of treatment for physical, emotional, or medical problems, without the advice of a physician. The author's intent is only to offer information of a general nature to help you in your quest for emotional, physical, and spiritual well-being.

In the event you use any of the information in this book, the author and the publisher assume no responsibility for your actions.

*This book is dedicated to my husband, Eric, who has
always believed in me, even when I have doubted myself,
and to my sons, Jacob and Josh, who fill
my life with love, laughter, and endless
inspiration to be a better human.*

CONTENTS

INTRODUCTION

Can we be real for a minute? Like, really real? The kind of real usually reserved for that friend you can text hilarious but slightly inappropriate parenting memes to (the ones you can't share on Facebook lest people question your parenting skills, but that are in fact hilarious)?

The type of real reserved for the friend you can tell anything—even your embarrassing stories, your deepest fears, and your secret dreams? Yeah, that kind of real.

You in? Okay, pull up a seat on my proverbial front porch, get comfy and let's talk. Overachiever to overachiever. Personal development junkie to personal development junkie . . .

This shit is hard! All of it. [gestures vaguely]

We've been given the herculean task of trying to simultaneously

- crush it at work;

- raise brilliant, kind, well-rounded humans;

- be an amazing, loving partner;

- give back to the community;

- have a social life and stay in touch with friends and family;

- manage our homes and all that entails;

- organize and execute plans with military precision so that all the kids can make all of their sports and activities, do their homework, and . . . *What? They need to be fed AGAIN!? Frick.*

- and not completely lose our minds in the process.

Oh, and here's a multiyear pandemic while you're at it, you know, just to make life more interesting. *May the odds be ever in your favor!*

But don't you dare let anyone see you struggling. Be a giver, not a taker. Pull up your big girl panties and get the job done and look good doing it. The contradictions and sky-high expectations never end.

It's a lot and we struggle because we're human. So what do we do? If you're like me, you turn to personal development and self-help books.

We assume there's some magical solution out there that can help us be the calm, confident human we want to be and not the hot mess who hides in the pantry eating chocolate, quietly crying and wondering why this is so hard and if we're the only ones struggling. (We're not.)

We buy the self-help guru's book with the very Zen cover (or maybe something with "F*ck It" in the title if we're feeling a bit salty that day), and we hope and pray it will give us the answers we're looking for. And sometimes we do find answers. A practice that brings us more peace in our days. A profound truth that takes our breath away and makes us think, *Yes, I am a frickin' Zen warrior! I've got this!* if only for a moment.

But more often than not what we get is advice that makes our eyes roll so hard we nearly black out because it's so ridiculously impractical.

Or even worse, the advice sounds like we *should* be able to manage it—if we really buckle down, get up at 5 a.m., and power through the exhaustion. After all, they say that if we want it badly enough, we'll do the work. *You're not uncommitted, are you? You said you wanted enlightenment, rock-hard abs, and a four-hour workweek, right? Well, buckle up, buttercup, and do the work!*

So we buckle up and we wake up at 5 a.m. (even though we got only six hours of sleep last night) and we try to empty our minds and tap into the universal consciousness, etc., etc.—even though all we can think about is how we can't comfortably sit criss-cross-applesauce-style anymore, and *Man, my back hurts* and *Oh crap, did I remember to get the clothes out of the dryer?* (No, no you did not.)

We repeat positive affirmations we only half believe, trying to improve our mindset. We tidy up our homes and donate anything that doesn't "spark joy"—only to find out that three kids later, even Marie Kondo had to admit that keeping a minimalistic, tidy house isn't exactly compatible with real life and a houseful of kids.

We don't need fads or fluff. We need to get back to common-sense basics and practical solutions.

Case in point, I took a burnout course recently and the woman suggested we should all ditch the alarm and just sleep until our bodies are ready to wake up. Which I guess would be awesome if you're either retired or self-employed and childless, but I don't think my kids' schools would appreciate it if I rolled up at 10 a.m., latte in hand, and said dreamily, "We just don't do alarms, sorry."

I'm pretty sure the truancy officer would be at my door real quick! Not to mention if you have, you know, a job and a boss who expects you to be in before noon, this type of advice is far from practical.

Some of it just makes me laugh, but some of it has made me cry in frustration, thinking, *What is wrong with me? Why can't I just follow the stupid 20-step plan to ultimate success and enlightenment like the childless billionaire dude told me he did?*

Well, lean in real close and I'll tell you a secret . . .

Most of it is BS grounded in neither reality nor science. We've been sold a bill of goods, and it's just not practical for the majority of us to follow the crazy advice that's out there.

Yes, maybe the childless billionaire with a big team and full-time house staff can keep up the complicated routines, but what about the rest of us? What about the busy moms who want abs of steel but also love cinnamon buns? What about the overachievers who want a successful career but also like to Netflix and (literally) chill some nights?

I mean, yes, I get that the average American watches four hours of TV a day and that equates to a decade of our lives lost to trash TV, but you won't hear me saying TV is the devil and to throw away the remote if you're serious about getting your life together.

I'm more the kind of gal who will tell you to cut back from four hours of TV to one hour and spend the other three hours getting real human connection and doing something fulfilling . . . *but also, if you've not yet, check out* Ted Lasso *because it is freakin' hilarious!*

Here's the thing: If you're anything like me, you're an overachiever and always have been. The risk of you completely checking out with Netflix and a big bottle of wine for four hours a day is probably pretty low. We've got too much we want to accomplish.

And we need some downtime. Both are true. We need to be able to shut off our brains for an hour and get lost in a good book or a good show, and we shouldn't be shamed for it.

This isn't about giving up and releasing personal responsibility, this is about leveraging advice that's actually grounded in reality and unlearning the junk that's been holding us back.

Stuart Smalley Was My Guru

A little context about me before we go on this book journey together . . .

I grew up on a farm in western Kentucky in a culture where hard work and grit were respected and expected. You showed up, worked hard, and got the job done. *Toughen up, don't be a crybaby, and for God's sake don't be lazy* was the vibe.

I was taught to always do my best—which in my mind meant going above and beyond. I got straight A's, was a "delight to have in class," and signed up for sports and volunteer activities to make sure my college application would be properly padded all the way back to middle school.

Did all this striving have me popping TUMS before school every day and crying over timed multiplication tables in fourth grade? Yes, yes it did. I also didn't know how *not* to worry so much or care any less, so what was a worrywart kid to do?

Hard work I knew, but personal development and self-growth? Well, the only example I had of that growing up was Stuart

Smalley on *Saturday Night Live*. You remember Stuart, right? The goofy guy with colorful sweaters who would sit in front of a full-length mirror and repeat his daily affirmations to himself. "I'm good enough, I'm smart enough, and doggone it, people like me!"

To this day, if I say anything remotely inspirational on Facebook, my big brother will drop a Stuart Smalley gif in the comments. Stuart was the personal development guru of our childhood, for better or worse.

With that as my only frame of reference, you can see how even the most basic self-help concepts felt like a foreign language when I stumbled into the world of personal development books back in 2013 as I was starting my business.

I always say that entrepreneurship is the greatest personal development journey I ever could have gone on, and it's true! To make it as an entrepreneur, you *have* to work on yourself. You have to deal with your mindset trash, because when you put yourself and your work out into the world, your limiting beliefs *will* try to smack you down. I was told that mindset work was the key to success, so like the nerdy good girl that I am, I dove in with enthusiasm.

I was enamored with this new way of seeing the world, and it made a big difference in my confidence. I started to see just how toxic my self-talk was and how important it was to change it. The books I read made a big impact on me, and I'm grateful for what I learned.

However, I also found some of the advice to be completely impractical or just plain too "out there" for me to comprehend or actually implement. I dared not admit that out loud, though, lest I be seen as uncommitted to doing the work or close-minded. I assumed if I wasn't seeing results, it meant something was wrong with me, not the methods being taught.

The truth is, some of the things that I find crazy and impractical work for some people—they just didn't work for me, and maybe they didn't work for you either—and that's okay.

What's not okay is being shamed and blamed if we don't find success with some guru's methodology. I see way too much of that out there. What's not okay is going into a shame spiral because we can't maintain someone else's idea of the perfect day or morning routine.

We've Been Making Things Way Too Complicated!

Here's the thing: We don't need a one-size-fits-all magic bullet solution. We need practical advice that works in the real world, not some self-proclaimed guru's 20-step plan that's impossible to implement. What we need is a simple and adaptable plan that can fit into our unique lifestyle.

The only problem with the fact that there is no magic bullet solution is that we really like magic bullets. We like a sexy app or a beautifully designed planner that promises to revolutionize our days. We want to be able to take a pill and get skinny and still eat the cake. We want it all, and we want it with same-day delivery, thank you very much.

I get it—me too—and I wish I could promise you that, but this isn't that kind of book. My job here isn't to give you a plan for a perfect day, or a cure-all. **My job is to uncomplicate things in an all-too-complicated world.**

We're not lacking advice, we're drowning in it. My goal here is to help you unlearn the BS that you didn't even realize was BS, to shift your perspective to something more helpful and empowering, and then arm you with practical, proven habits you can actually use to better your life.

I don't claim to have it all figured out. I'm not a doctor, therapist, neuroscientist, or research scientist. What I am is a smart cookie who's read bookshelves full of personal development books, taken countless courses and coaching certifications, and read research studies that made my eyes cross and light up with new clarity all at the same time. I've experimented, succeeded, flopped, and taken field notes along the way for the past 10 years.

I'm a Certified High Performance Coach and have built a successful business over the past decade, and I'm proud of the solid reputation I've built along the way as someone who serves with compassion, honesty, and wholeheartedness. Maybe even more importantly, I'm a busy parent like you, a book nerd, a neuroscience geek, and the kind of person who won't give you some BS strategy that I know is going to make you feel like a failure in a week because it's just not sustainable.

Honestly, we tend to make this stuff way too complicated. We overthink it and believe that if it's not packaged up in a fancy system with a cool name, it probably won't work for us.

The reality is that more often than not we don't need *more* to do, we need less. We need to strip away the trappings and uncomplicate things.

We need to get back to basics and common sense. The reality is that common sense is not always common practice.

Warning!

I'll warn you right now that some of what I share in this book will seem so basic, you'll be tempted to skim over it. You'll be tempted to think, *I know this, I've heard it before* and want to skip ahead. Don't. *That's* what got us into this mess in the first place—thinking, *Yeah, yeah, yeah, I've got it, tell me something new. Give me something fancy and shiny. Dazzle me!*

Anytime you catch yourself thinking that, remind yourself, "Common sense isn't always common practice," and that you're way too smart to ignore commonsense practices. Don't discount something just because it seems basic. It might be basic, but are you doing it? Consistently? Be honest.

There's a Better Way

I think we've all tried to overhaul our entire lives in one fell swoop, only to come crashing down from our self-growth high a few weeks later and realize we can't keep up the pace.

And when that happens, we tend to use the same all-or-nothing mentality that got us into this mess to justify throwing our hands in the air and saying, "Screw it! If I can't work out for 60 minutes daily, cut out processed foods, meal prep every Sunday, meditate for an hour, get eight hours of sleep, and start a new business at the same time, then what kind of loser am I, anyway? Pass the tacos and margaritas! I give up!"

Now, although I appreciate a hard-won rant and a margarita as much as the next woman, I do believe there's a better way.

First, you need to unlearn some things that you may have never second-guessed before but are in fact a load of bull and aren't helping you out. We need to call out not only the BS being fed to us by society but also our own BS, no matter how uncomfortable. (We've got this, I promise!)

Next, we need to uncomplicate things, get back to basics, and start focusing on what actually makes a difference. You'll be amazed at the impact just a few good habits and a good ol' reality check can make on your life. In fact, that's the key to unlocking better days, less stress, and more success.

You ready? Let's go!

Final note: To respect the privacy of my clients, I've changed their names while sharing their stories. However, I want to assure you that all the stories are true and reflect real-life experiences.

LIAR, LIAR, PANTS ON FIRE!

The greatest obstacle to discovery is
not ignorance—it is the illusion of knowledge.

DANIEL J. BOORSTIN

The first step on our journey to living our best lives (whatever that means to you) is unlearning a whole lot of stuff that's just not serving us and is in fact holding us back.

In this section, we're going to dive into unlearning what we think we know about overachieving, willpower, hustle, and the idea that stress is the enemy. (Spoiler alert: It's not.) We're also going to tackle the idea that we need to know it all and that sacrificing our own needs is the only way to succeed.

Let's face it: Some of these beliefs and habits aren't doing us any favors. Some are straight up lies we've been told by society and misinformed thought leaders. We need to let go of what's not serving us and make room for new ways of showing up that actually work. So get ready to challenge some assumptions and be open to new perspectives. It's time to unlearn a few things so we can unleash our full potential!

Chapter 1

SORRY, BUT "HIGH ACHIEVER" IS NOT A BADGE OF HONOR

*Unhappiness is not knowing what we want
and killing ourselves to get it.*
DON HEROLD

If you're anything like me, at some point you've probably said with pride that you're an overachiever. When you did, it probably felt like you were listing a really admirable personality trait—like being honest, generous, or kind.

You probably had a shelf full of trophies and awards growing up, always made the honor roll, and volunteered on the weekends. It felt good. You were proud of yourself, and rightly so.

This trend continued when you graduated and joined the workforce. Stellar reviews from your boss, commending you for all the late nights and weekends you put in to get a big project done on time. You raised your hand every time an opportunity came up so you could prove yourself. You quickly became the go-to person at the office. You always go above and beyond.

And then there's all the extra stuff—PTA president, snack provider at soccer games, and car-pool coordinator for the half a dozen sports and activities your kids are in.

When people ask how you do it all, you just smile and shrug it off like it's no big deal. It might be a point of pride, but it is also a source of exhaustion. It makes you feel like Supergirl—but also like there might be some kryptonite secretly hidden in your purse, draining the life out of you.

You're striving, and in a lot of ways you're crushing it—but you're also being crushed under the weight of it all. Cracks are starting to appear—chinks in your armor.

One day you realize you're not as patient with the kids as you want to be. You're snapping at your partner and running your home like a drill sergeant—but *hey, somebody has to keep everyone on time and organized. You're welcome, everybody!*

We can keep this up for years and assume that this is just how life is and there's no other way. We say we're *fine* and push through the hard days. We stay up a little too late so that we can *finally* have some precious alone time and a well-earned glass of wine to help us wind down before bed. The days start to run together and we have a nagging sense that surely there's more to life, but we can't really put our finger on it, and hey, we've got it pretty good, we can't complain. Right? So we soldier on even though we feel like we're on autopilot and somewhat checked out of our own lives.

I did this for years. I thought this was just life with kids, and what else was I going to do anyway? Especially once my business hit a certain level of success and I had so many of the things that had once only been dreams on my vision board.

My husband and I got married right after college, and for years we were barely scraping by. We couldn't afford cable TV, took a sack lunch to work every day, and would get free trial after free trial of AOL to be able to enjoy the internet at home. (I know, I'm definitely showing my age with that last one.)

Fast-forward 20 years and I was making six figures per year working from home with my rescue dogs by my feet. I was literally living the introvert's dream life! We had a great house and good friends, took nice vacations, and had basically everything we wanted.

How could I possibly complain about anything? It felt ungrateful, and that felt like a mortal sin, so I gritted my teeth and got on with it. I worked the long hours, didn't get out much, and started to pack on some extra weight. *This is what your 30s and 40s are supposed to look like, right?*

What I didn't know then but fully believe now is that chasing your dreams shouldn't come with collateral damage to your health, happiness, and relationships.

There is a better way, but I didn't even know to look for it. And then the pandemic hit in 2020. Pre-pandemic I was already working 50-hour weeks and feeling stretched too thin. Pandemic life was like throwing gasoline on a fire.

You see, I've struggled with anxiety my entire life—I was what they called a "worrywart" kid, and I had ulcers to show for it by second grade. I always felt like there was something wrong with me. I was too sensitive and cared way too much about, well, everything.

Since I'd been anxious my whole life, I was used to it. It was just part of my personality, and it didn't hold me back from doing (most of) the things I wanted to do. Until it did.

The pandemic was the straw that broke the camel's back. Although I had gotten used to a certain level of stress and anxiety over the years, this "new normal," as the news was fond of calling it, was more than I could handle.

My 10-hour workdays turned into 12-hour days, thanks to the constant interruptions that come with having two kids at home doing remote learning for an entire year, including an eight-year-old with then-undiagnosed attention-deficit hyperactivity disorder.

Josh, my youngest son, was camped out in our dining room right across from my home office when remote learning began. Josh isn't a quiet child—he's one of those kids who seems to be yelling all the time and doesn't really have an inside voice. At first, he didn't have headphones, but all the chatter was way too distracting for me. Once he did get headphones, I couldn't hear his classmates, but what I could hear was Josh yelling out random things throughout the day.

The answer is 57!

Christopher Columbus!

It's a verb!

Is that your cat?

When's break time?

It might have been hilarious if it hadn't been so distracting and I hadn't been so exhausted. And don't even get me started with the tech problems. It felt like the world was on fire, but I was just supposed to pretend that it was all manageable. I still had a job to do and people depending on me. So I still got the work done, even if it meant working 12-hour days. I showed up with a smile on my face and a good attitude and helped people.

And then I'd log off and quietly cry between meetings, hiding behind my monitor so my family couldn't hear or see me breaking down. What they could see, though, was me losing my patience and yelling at them over silly, insignificant things. I was suddenly a very unhappy person, but I had no idea what I was so mad about or what to do about it. When something has to give, unfortunately, the people who love us most tend to get the worst of us. It wasn't a conscious decision, I just couldn't hold it together 24/7. It still really sucks and comes with a ton of mom guilt, though—that's collateral damage.

Sometimes I would make it through the day without crying at my desk, but then I'd lie down at night and have a full-blown panic attack and feel like I was dying. Eventually I would get a diagnosis of severe anxiety and mild depression.

I was overwhelmed and drowning, but so was everyone else, so no one really noticed. They were fighting their own battles. No one was going to save me. I had to save myself, so I got busy finding answers.

If it hadn't been for the pandemic, had I not hit my breaking point, I might have gone on burning the candle at both ends for years, thinking there was no other option, no better way.

I would have kept working the long hours, losing my patience with the people I love most, and feeling like a head without a body, I was so checked out. I was comfortably numb, as Pink Floyd says, but resigned to this way of living.

I still would have told you I was an overachiever. I could have pointed to everything I'd accomplished and even called myself a high achiever. What I've come to learn, however, is that there's a big difference between high achievement and high performance. What I know now is that I want to be a high performer instead.

The Difference Between High Achievement and High Performance

Brendon Burchard is the founder of the High Performance Institute and the world's highest-paid performance coach. He has paved the way with research into what it means to be a high performer since the early 2000s.

In his book *High Performance Habits*, Burchard defines high performance as "succeeding beyond standard norms, consistently over the long term, while still maintaining positive well-being and relationships." He goes on to say that this "requires habits that protect your well-being, maintain positive relationships, and ensure that you serve others as you climb. . . . It's about creating a high performance life, in which you experience an ongoing feeling of full engagement, joy, and confidence that comes from being your best self."[1]

In short, if you're successful but not also joyful, fully present, and making your health and well-being a top priority—then you're not a high performer. You might be a high achiever and an overachiever, but you're not a high performer.

I don't know about you, but I don't *just* want to be successful; I also want to be happy and healthy. I want to feel like I'm being the best parent I know how to be, a loving and supportive partner, and a good friend. When people ask me what my hobbies are, I don't want to give them a blank look and mumble something about *not really having any free time.*

That's why I went straight to the source, the High Performance Institute, and became a Certified High Performance Coach. High performance isn't reserved just for elite athletes or workaholic CEOs running start-ups in Silicon Valley.

High performance is for everyone who wants to be wildly successful *and* actually enjoy their lives—not just in some far-off retirement stage, but in the here and now. Not only is the future not guaranteed, but if we're careless with our personal lives while we're making all that money, we might not have anyone who wants to hang out with us by the time we reach retirement age!

With that in mind, it's time to unlearn everything we thought we knew about achievement and what it means to be successful. If all that striving comes with collateral damage to our relationships and life, we shouldn't want it. Let's be high performers instead.

Chapter 2

WILLPOWER WON'T KEEP YOU FROM EATING THE THIN MINTS

Don't rely on willpower. It's unreliable. Make a plan and create an environment that supports your goals.
MEL ROBBINS

Willpower doesn't work. On some level, we all know this. We've all tried to use willpower to change our lives, only to drop our New Year's resolutions as soon as Girl Scout cookie season rolls around. *Ahh, Thin Mints, my childhood love and my annual diet nemesis, we meet again!*

We've sworn to stop checking our phones so much, only to realize we've mindlessly picked it up, again, and have been scrolling Facebook for the last 10 minutes. *D'oh!*

While I'm all for taking personal responsibility, relying on willpower alone to achieve our goals is not a solid strategy. Willpower can be a fickle friend. That's why in this book, we're going to dive into some alternative ways to reach our goals. Sure, grit and determination are admirable qualities, but on their own, they're not enough to create the lasting change we crave.

Think about it. We live in a world full of temptations—we literally have the entire internet in the palm of our hands, and social media is crafted by the world's best engineers to be highly addictive. It's a dopamine hit fest. We can get food and alcohol delivered right to our doorstep, and Netflix is infinitely more interesting than doing housework or writing a report.

We've got culturally accepted addictions out the wazoo, and they are way too much for a mere mortal to resist 100 percent of the time. That's why if we're relying solely on willpower to create awesome lives, we're doomed. We need some help.

We've been told that if we're not buckling down and just doing the damn thing already, then we don't want it badly enough and simply don't have what it takes. *But is that true?*

Sure, performance necessity (the feeling that we "must" succeed) is an important ingredient of success, but we can't *just* want to succeed; we should also be creating conditions that make success inevitable rather than a heroic effort.

Now, willpower is not entirely useless, but the key is to leverage your limited willpower supply strategically, focusing on the areas where it can make the most difference.

For instance, you can use your willpower to create routines that reinforce your goals, such as setting aside a specific time for meal-prepping on weekends to make eating healthfully easier during the week. By doing this, you essentially "automate" the positive habit and no longer need to rely on willpower to maintain it.

Additionally, you can use willpower to take small, incremental steps toward your goals. Instead of trying to make massive changes all at once (like giving up all processed foods cold turkey), focus on making one positive choice at a time (like trading Thin Mints for dark chocolate). By concentrating your willpower on these smaller decisions, you are more likely to succeed and build momentum toward your ultimate goal.

In short, although willpower alone won't guarantee success, it can be a valuable tool when used in conjunction with other strategies.

The Power of Our Environment

Environmental design is one such strategy. The basic idea is that we can outsource the need for willpower to our environment to set ourselves up for success.

When I say environment here, I am referring to your physical environment, but also to the people you surround yourself with, the information you fill your head with, and the food you're consuming that fuels your body. They all influence our habits and actions.

The need for environmental design makes sense when you think about it. If you've got a pantry full of Thin Mints but no fruits and veggies, it's going to be *really* hard to say no to the Thin Mints and eat healthfully.

If getting to the gym feels as difficult as an hour-long trek in the snow "uphill both ways," as the saying goes, it's going to be really easy to make excuses and just stay at home snug in bed instead of heading out the door in the morning.

Far too often, we make things harder than they have to be and try to white-knuckle it instead of making the default option our desired option.

When we wander into the pantry or sit down at our desks to work, the easy option to choose should be the one that will get us to where we want to be—one step closer to our goals—not Thin Mints or an endless Facebook feed.

Why Are We Like This?

Why do we cling to grit and willpower when environmental design could be our secret weapon? Well, it's probably because we've been raised to believe in individualism and that hard work is the only path to success.

Here's the thing: Our potential is actually shaped more by our environment, which can both challenge and support us. Let me explain . . .

Historian Will Durant discovered that the heroes we look up to became great not because of innate qualities like willpower or grit, but because they faced tough situations that shaped them. Their environment demanded greatness, and they rose to the challenge.

That means greatness isn't about having some sort of magical superhero genes; it's about being in the right environment that pushes us to excel. That's good news, right?

We can stop relying on willpower and instead focus on creating environments that push us while also giving us space to rest and recharge. The best part is, we don't have to shoulder the weight of our challenges all by ourselves. We can share the load with our environment. *Now, doesn't that feel like a breath of fresh air?*

It's all about finding that sweet spot—pushing ourselves, tackling challenges, and cultivating environments that help us flourish. We need to embrace new information, experiences, rest, and relationships, and we need to ensure our surroundings support that.

Harvard psychologist Ellen Langer puts it perfectly: "Social psychologists argue that who we are at any one time depends mostly on the context in which we find ourselves. But who creates the context? The more mindful we are, the more we can create the contexts we are in . . . and believe in the possibility of change."[2]

In section 3, we'll talk more about how exactly we can use environmental design to our advantage. For now, just know that willpower isn't the key to success and never has been. It's time to unlearn this misguided concept once and for all.

Chapter 3

DO THE HUSTLE (OR, YOU KNOW, DON'T)

You can't hustle your way to enoughness.
HILARY RUSHFORD

We've already discussed how problematic being an over-achiever and trying to check all the boxes of success can be if you're not doing it in a healthy, high-performance way. Now it's time to unlearn a few things about hustle culture.

Why does hustle culture get its own chapter? Is it not the same thing as overachieving? In my mind—no. Although there's a lot of overlap in the issues that arise from overachieving and hustle culture, I want to make a distinction that's specifically about the concept of hustling.

Whereas overachievement is about striving to accomplish big things at the expense of other areas of our lives, hustling is that nasty little habit of staying busy for the sake of staying busy.

That need to always be doing and going and filling our lives to overflowing—just so we don't have to stop and be with ourselves. Just so we can feel like we matter. "I do, therefore I am" is the motto of hustle culture.

We wear busyness like a badge. How many times this month has someone asked you how you're doing and you've responded with "I'm great! Busy, but great!"

Does catching up with your friends often involve a low-key contest of who's the busiest? "OMG, there's so much going on! There's just not enough time in the day!"

Farm Girl Meets Entrepreneurship

Hustle culture may seem like a more modern trend, but the idea of pushing ourselves to the limit with long work hours has been around for centuries. The driving forces behind it are complex and interconnected, spanning economic factors, societal expectations, social comparison, and technology.

As I mentioned earlier, I grew up in a blue-collar farming culture where hard work and grit were revered and laziness was frowned upon. When you live on a farm, there's always something that needs to be done, and everyone needs to pitch in. Whether that's mowing for three hours every summer weekend, feeding animals, or stacking firewood in the winter, there's always work to be done, and even being the baby of the family won't get you a pass from working.

So I already had the whole hard work thing bred into me, but then there was the hustle culture, which was much revered back in 2013 when I started my business.

Entrepreneur Gary Vaynerchuk was a big deal at the time, and even if you were working 10-hour days, listening to even two minutes of his videos could have you walking away feeling like a total slacker. His motto was basically "You can rest when you die!" and "If you aren't sacrificing your life at the altar of business success, then you probably should go ahead and turn in your entrepreneur card, because you aren't going to cut it around here."

Although it was a common mindset at the time, it always rubbed me the wrong way. Far too aggressive for my taste—and yet, it made me question myself and fed into my fears.

What if he's right and I'm not committed enough? What if I'm being too sensitive? Success does take sacrifice. Am I doing enough? Giving enough? Am I enough?

And that, my friend, is the crux of it. *Am I enough?*

You won't find the answer by hustling, though. You can't hustle your way to enoughness.

How much money do you have to make per year to call yourself successful enough?

How many awards and accolades and followers on social media do you need to feel enough?

I hate to break it to you, but no one out there is going to step forward and crown you "enough" someday. And you—well, even if you set the goalpost, I can guarantee that once you get there, you'll move it. You'll just keep chasing a moving target, never feeling like you're enough.

Until you choose it for yourself. Until you decide you are enough. Just as you are, no disclaimers needed. No if/then statement to complete.

You are enough.

I honestly don't believe there's a person alive who hasn't struggled with this. Not feeling "enough" is at the heart of almost every limiting belief. Every shitty story we tell ourselves that holds us back from going for what we really want.

Whether it presents as "pretty enough" or "smart enough" or "lovable enough" or "rich enough" or a dozen other things, not feeling like we're enough seems to be at the heart of most of our struggles.

Although I doubt I can convince you in these pages that you're already enough and already worthy of all you desire (you are), what I want you to really believe, deep in your bones, is that you can't hustle your way to enoughness.

Hustle isn't the answer. Hustle is a coping mechanism.

I'm Drowning! Give Me More!

It took me a long time to figure this out, but looking back, it is painfully obvious how often I've used busyness as an unhealthy coping mechanism rather than facing my fears and doing the hard work of addressing my real problems.

Once again, the pandemic provides me with the perfect example . . .

Remember how by the end of 2020 I was so overwhelmed that I was having severe anxiety, crying every day, and having panic attacks almost nightly? I was coming apart at the seams, so you would think that I would have scaled back and done less wherever possible, right?

I wish. Since I had no clue how to cope in healthy ways, what I did instead was foster two dogs for local rescue groups—a wild-child puppy followed by a big dog recovering from hip surgery that needed time to recover.

But wait, there's more! I didn't stop at fostering needy dogs (even though I already had three dogs and a cat of my own). I also started an e-commerce business as a passion project, took a class to learn how to paint abstract art, and then proceeded to sell several paintings to friends and family around the country.

And then the biggest commitment of all (which I don't regret because it ultimately changed my life) was signing up for a nine-month-long coaching certification program. *I mean, what else are you supposed to do when you're struggling with anxiety and depression and completely overwhelmed during a pandemic?*

You see, when I finally admitted that I needed help and wasn't going to get myself out of the mental hell I was living in on my own, I did two things: I started medication for anxiety and depression and I hired a therapist who could meet with me online since we were still in lockdown.

I don't regret either of those choices. I am a big believer in using whatever tools you need to improve your mental health and well-being, and the meds helped me find a sense of calm so that I could catch my breath again. I also knew I didn't want to take them long term because of some other health concerns. So even though the meds saved me in many ways, I knew I wanted to get off of them as soon as possible.

And then there's therapy. Again, I think therapy can be wonderful for many issues and the world would probably be a much better place if everyone went to therapy at least for a while sometime in their lives. The therapy sessions helped me work through some of the fears that were driving my panic and sense of hopelessness, and yet my overall sense of anxiety was still there, simmering beneath the surface.

In fact, at one point I had a panic attack *during* a therapy session. What I came to realize (thanks to the coaching certification program) was that my nervous system was too dysregulated to handle it. I didn't feel safe in my body and was living in a constant state of fight or flight. When you're in fight-or-flight mode, the rational, reasoning part of your brain isn't as accessible, and it's hard to get the full benefit of therapy when you're in that state.

I'll cover the nervous system regulation piece in more detail later, but for now, let's get back to why unlearning hustle culture is so important.

Busyness as a Coping Mechanism

Busyness doesn't have to look as extreme as it did for me during the pandemic. We can hide behind busyness in everyday small ways like playing on our phones while simultaneously watching TV and mindlessly stuffing chips in our mouths because we crave the constant dopamine hits that come with swiping and liking and commenting while also catching up on that new hit show.

God forbid we should just sit and watch the show and allow ourselves to get sucked into that world for a while. *If you think that's hard, try sitting with your thoughts for a while—no phone, no TV, no distractions. Yikes.*

It reminds me of a meme I once saw that said, "I saw a guy at the coffee shop just sitting there drinking his coffee. No phone or laptop, just sitting there, like a psychopath."

I had to laugh when I read it because that scenario would be rare indeed! If we looked up from our phones long enough to even notice the psycho, he would probably stick out like a sore thumb.

In theory, our lives are full. In reality, they're empty when we're living like this. In the 21st century, the most rebellious thing we can do is to take some time every day to unplug and be with our thoughts and the world around us. The real world, not a screen. Our real thoughts and dreams and desires, not our worry thoughts or what someone else is telling us is important.

Unlearning hustle culture and the habit of using busyness as a coping mechanism can revolutionize our lives if we let it. In section 3, I'll show you how to put this into practice, but for now, just start getting comfy with the reality that you can't hustle your way to enoughness—you're already enough.

Yes, you. Really.

Chapter 4

STRESS, THE MISJUDGED VILLAIN (IT'S TIME FOR A RE-TRIAL)

The best way to manage stress isn't to reduce or avoid it,
but rather to rethink and even embrace it.
KELLY McGONIGAL

You want to talk about getting a bad rep that you don't deserve? Well, move over, Severus Snape, stress is the king of this!

Watch the news or hit up Google, and you will be hard-pressed to find anything positive about stress. In fact, 99.9 percent of the results will be about how stress is killing you and how to avoid it. Take, for example . . .

"Stress Is America's #1 Health Problem"—The American Institute of Stress

"Stress Is Responsible for 75–90% of All Doctor's Visits"

"Stress Is a Silent Killer"

"Stress Is Contagious—Here's How to Protect Yourself"

"Nine Ways Stress Is More Dangerous Than You Think"

Stress feels like the ultimate villain. It's easy to get stressed about stress when we feel like it's out to get us!

Case in point: In 2022 I landed my first national TV interview on a show called *The List.* My segment was called "Three Daily Rituals to Eliminate Stress." To say that I was stressed about my first TV interview would be an understatement. I was so nervous, I felt like I might puke before I joined the reporter on Zoom. I was grateful it wasn't in a TV studio so they couldn't see me gripping my sweaty palms together under my desk. And the worst part? I felt like a fraud! I was about to tell a national audience how to deal with their stress, but I couldn't calm myself down?! It was embarrassing.

Here's the thing: The tips I shared during that interview are solid tips, and I still stand behind them. The problem was that they were all based on the idea that stress is a problem to solve by calming down. Although we absolutely do need strategies to calm our nervous system and get ourselves into a regulated state (more on this later), we also need to know how to leverage stress and use it to our advantage.

It's a case of needing the right tool for the job. A hammer is great for driving in a nail, but it won't do us much good if we need to saw a board in half.

What I didn't know at the time of *The List* interview was that although nervous system regulation techniques are amazing tools, they're not the only tools I need in my tool kit. Sometimes we don't need to push the stress down—we need to lean into it. Let me explain . . .

Back in 2013, Kelly McGonigal, PhD, gave a TED Talk about how to make stress your friend.[3] When I first heard about it, the very idea seemed laughable.

Make stress my friend? Are you kidding me? Stress had been my nemesis since second grade! I hated stress! It made me sweat before big presentations, had caused me to play it safe and small on numerous occasions so that I missed out on cool stuff I really wanted to do—and have you seen those headlines about how stress is a killer?

It was like suggesting I cozy up with Jack the Ripper. *No thanks, crazy lady!* But then I listened to the talk and eventually read her book *The Upside of Stress*. Turns out Kelly is a brilliant researcher and not, in fact, a crazy lady. *Go figure!*

I wish I could say that when I heard her TED Talk back in 2013, I really got this concept that stress isn't my enemy and how to leverage it in my day-to-day life. But it's funny how our brains will home in on the part that serves us most at that moment, even if it means we miss the rest of the message, which is what I did.

What is clear to me now is that McGonigal made two very important points and we need them both to really thrive.

At the time, the part of her talk that I really latched on to was something she said at the end, in response to a question: "Chasing meaning is better for your health than trying to avoid discomfort. . . . Go after what it is that creates meaning in your life and then trust yourself to handle the stress that follows."

I latched on to that part of her speech because at the time I was working a full-time job and running my business on the side. I desperately wanted to quit my job but was still working up the courage to take the leap and quit. Fueled by the idea that I didn't want to have any regrets and that I'd rather try and fail than never try at all, those few words from McGonigal fueled my convictions.

What I took away was that I should do the big scary thing because, yeah, it's stressful, but I can handle it. I was going to chase meaning, stress be damned! And that's what I did.

Chasing Meaning

I didn't completely appreciate what a big deal this concept is at the time, so let's take a moment to really dig into why chasing meaning is so important.

As a coach and consultant who's worked with entrepreneurs for a full decade now, often hearing the behind-the-scenes stories of running a business that you won't find on social media, I've seen this unfold time and time again.

Picture, for example, an entrepreneur who's making millions per year in revenue, with her business running like a well-oiled machine, so much so that she's barely needed for day-to-day operations. She's living the dream, right? This is the life she always wanted, and now it's a reality. *So why is she so bored? So disengaged? So dissatisfied with her life and business?*

It might sound crazy, but I've seen variations of this play out countless times during my coaching career. It could be tempting to brush this scenario off with a sarcastic *"Oh boo-freaking-hoo, rich girl. Some of us have real problems!,"* but while it's what I'd call a good problem to have, it's still a genuine issue.

Achieving wild success but still feeling dissatisfied is the type of problem we feel guilty complaining about. We hesitate to even ask for help; I mean, it's a first-world problem, right?

Well, it might be a first-world problem, but it's a problem nonetheless. Why? Because we need meaningful pursuits to feel alive and fulfilled. Humans thrive when we have goals to work toward and dreams to chase, and we languish when they're missing.

So, what do you do when you've reached your goals but feel adrift in the world? You start dreaming again and set new goals that excite you.

Going back to our successful entrepreneur, she could find a way to get more involved with the day-to-day operations of her business. Reconnecting to the work and her clients might be enough to get her excited about her mission again. She could also consider using her knowledge to mentor disadvantaged youth and teach them valuable entrepreneurial skills. In doing so, she would continue to chase meaning and set new goals while still being grateful for and appreciating her accomplishments.

Although we absolutely need to take some time to celebrate and appreciate life when we've reached our goals, we're not crazy to then set another goal and a next level to strive for. If we don't, we risk living a life spent in ho-hum harmony instead of a life that makes us want to jump out of bed in the morning.

Be grateful, yes, but the solution isn't to just be grateful for what you have, count your blessings, and stay put. The answer is to be grateful and keep going. Keep striving. Dare to dream bigger, even if it scares you, and trust yourself to handle it.

Chasing meaning is better for your health than trying to avoid discomfort was the first big idea from McGonigal's TED Talk. Now let's dive into her second eye-opening idea: why stress doesn't have to be our enemy.

Stress Is Not the Enemy

McGonigal spent a lot of years studying stress and touring the country, telling people about how stress is killing them and why they needed to get a handle on it. But then she came across a study that stopped her in her tracks. It made her question everything she thought she knew about stress and everything she'd been sharing over the years. Apparently, we've had it all wrong. Stress wasn't the bad guy after all. It was more like the misunderstood loner who got framed.

Here's why: It turns out that it's not the stress that's killing us— it's our beliefs about stress that are the real troublemakers.

Let me say that again: Stress isn't the real problem—it's the way we've been thinking about stress that's the problem. *Mind-blowing, right?*

In her TED Talk, McGonigal shares the research study[4] that changed everything for her. This study tracked 30,000 adults for eight years, and researchers started by asking people two questions:

1. How much stress have you experienced in the past year?

2. Do you believe that stress is harmful to your health?

Then they used public death records to find out who died. Morbid, I know, but here's where it gets interesting, so stick with me.

First, the bad news, and it's probably *not* going to surprise you: People who had experienced a lot of stress in the previous year had a 43 percent increased risk of dying—*but* that was true only for the people who *also* believed that stress is harmful to your health.

People who experienced a lot of stress but did *not* view stress as harmful were no more likely to die. In fact, they had the lowest risk of dying of anyone in the study, including those who had reported relatively little stress.

The researchers concluded that it wasn't stress alone that was killing people; it was a combination of stress and the belief that stress is harmful. They estimated that over 20,000 deaths per year are caused by the belief that stress is harmful to your health—not stress itself! That would make this *belief* the 15th leading cause of death in the United States, killing more people than skin cancer, HIV/AIDS, and homicide.

That's wild, right? It seems almost impossible to believe, but science backs up the findings. When you change your mind about stress, you can change your body's response to stress. Literally.

One of the big reasons stress is considered bad for our health is that when we get stressed, our heart rate goes up and our blood vessels constrict. That constriction is one of the reasons chronic stress is associated with cardiovascular disease—it's not healthy to stay in that state all the time. But in a separate study, Harvard researchers[5] found that when we view stress as helpful, our blood vessels actually stay relaxed—minimizing the effect of stress on our health.

Okay, so number one, this is such an amazing example of how our mindset can have real-world, tangible effects on our lives, right? And number two, this is great news, because it means we have much more control over the impact stress has on our health than we thought. How we think about stress matters, and it matters a lot. The good news is, we can change how we think about it.

Take 2

So how does this play out in the real world? Well, when I had that interview with *The List*, I knew a bunch of strategies to calm myself down, but when they didn't completely eliminate my stress, I started to stress about my stress, making everything worse. The negative self-talk kicked in, and I started to spiral. I couldn't calm down, and I ended up not being nearly as calm and collected as I had hoped to be. The story has a happy ending, though. The interview with *The List* was edited before it went on air and you can't tell how nervous I was when you watch the final product. They made it work.

Not only that but by the time my next TV interview rolled around, I had rediscovered the TED Talk by McGonigal and really heard what she was saying about stress mindsets this time, beyond the part about chasing meaning. I bought her book *The Upside of Stress* and went all in on understanding how to make friends with my stress.

My interview on *Good Morning Washington* was higher stakes and higher stress in every way—but this time, I nailed it because I had a secret weapon. I knew how to use stress to my advantage.

The reason I say it was higher stakes and higher stress is that when I showed up for the interview, I thought I was doing a segment for moms called "The Mother Side," which has more of a casual conversation vibe to it with one female anchor asking the questions. I also thought the segment was going to be recorded and air a few days later. I was wrong on both counts!

I quickly realized while waiting in the online equivalent of a green room that (a) I was going to be on live TV and masterful editing couldn't save me this time and (b) I was on the DC-area morning show with two anchors asking me questions, not on "The Mother Side."

I will admit this realization really got my heart rate up, but fortunately, I had a few moments to compose myself while watching the interview before mine. And this time, I knew my goal wasn't to calm down completely but to use stress to my advantage.

You see, because we've been taught to think of stress as the enemy, anytime we start sweating and feeling our hearts race we believe our bodies are betraying us and think, *You traitor! Why are you doing this to me?* We feel like we have some sort of fatal flaw and aren't cut out for this. That's definitely what I was feeling during *The List* interview and why I was freaking out. Now I knew better, and I told myself a different story.

I told myself that my pounding heart was a good sign—it was my body preparing me for something important. It was getting more oxygen to my brain so I could think more clearly and be fast on my feet as they asked me questions. I was hyperfocused on what I was doing and fully present, and I was prepared for this. It might not have been the scenario I was expecting, but I knew the points I wanted to make and had done my homework.

And maybe the most important part: I didn't tell myself I was a fraud for feeling some stress before sharing on live TV about stress—I just cared a whole hell of a lot about doing a good job, and that's nothing to be ashamed of. We stress about things we care about, and if you want to live a meaningful life and do important things you care about, you're going to have stress.

The goal isn't a stress-free life—the goal is to live a meaningful life and learn tools to help you handle the stress that will inevitably come up along the way.

I'll wrap up with a story McGonigal shares in her book *The Upside of Stress* that really stuck with me.[6] One night a psychologist, Alia Crum, was in her lab at Yale working late on a research project when the department's IT guy came in. Upon seeing her there toiling away, he said, "Just another cold, dark night on the side of Everest," and then turned and left.

It left her a little confused—it's not every night that the IT guy comes in and interrupts your work with a quote worthy of Confucius, but it stuck with her. Later, lying in bed, she realized just how profound and perfectly timed this comment was.

She had really been struggling under the weight of completing her dissertation and was telling herself a whole lot of unhelpful stories about what the struggle meant about her. The self-doubt was making everything harder.

What the man's words made her realize was that her dissertation was her own personal Everest. When you sign up to climb Mount Everest, you know going in that it's not going to be easy—that's not why you choose to do it. You know it's going to be hard. There will be times you want to give up, when you're sitting in the cold and dark on the side of the mountain and think you must have been out of your mind to attempt it. But surely you must also be thinking, *Well, this is what I signed up for. I signed up for a challenge—to do big things, not for a walk in the park.*

You're not sitting in your tent thinking, *What a load of BS! I didn't think this would be so hard! Get me out of here! Waaah!*

You and I might never climb Mount Everest, but we have our own personal Everests just like Alia Crum. Whether it's running a business, leading a team, or raising our kids, we all have our challenges. It's not sunshine and rainbows all the time. More often than not we experience a whole lot of frostbite and avalanches along the way, metaphorically speaking. But it means something to us and it's worthwhile, so we keep going. We might grumble a little, but we signed up for this, and we've got what it takes.

In section 3, I'll give you some practical tips on how to regulate your nervous system, but for now, here's a way to remind yourself that stress isn't the enemy and you're on the right track if you're chasing meaning: Give yourself a physical reminder.

We're human and we sometimes forget, while slogging up the mountain, why we started in the first place. Write "Everest" on a sticky note and stick it to your computer monitor so you see it every day. Or find a necklace, bracelet, or key chain with a mountain on it. Make a poster and put it on your wall—whatever you decide to do, find something to remind yourself that you're on the right path and some cold, dark nights are worth it.

Chapter 5

IT'S NOT SELFISH, IT'S SELF-PRESERVATION

*You are not required to set yourself on fire
to keep other people warm.*
UNKNOWN

Be honest: How many times has a scenario like this played out in your life?

Things are going pretty well—you've been getting enough sleep for a change, work is going well, and you feel like you finally have the whole work-life balance thing figured out. *Score!*

But then one of the kids gets sick and starts showing up at your bedside every hour. All night long. For a week. Now you're tired and trying to work from home while taking care of them. You don't have time to meal prep and cook, because they're clinging to you like a baby koala. Even if you can peel them off you for an hour, you're playing catch-up with work and are way too tired to exercise or do anything else for yourself.

A week goes by and they're healthy and back to school (yay!), but now you're off your routine. You haven't worked out, eaten healthy, or gotten eight hours of sleep in a week and can't summon the willpower to get back on track, so you slip-slide your way back to your old habits and routines instead, barely aware of what's happening.

I can't tell you how many times this scenario, or a similar one, has played out in my own life, and I don't think I'm alone in this. Let's face it: When things go sideways, our own needs tend to take a back seat and all our healthful habits tend to go out the window—even though they're what we need most in tough times. It's got to stop!

Now, I'm not saying that we should leave our kids to fend for themselves, but what I am saying is that our self-care can't go out the window every time life throws us a curveball.

How often have you felt like garbage and known exactly what you need to do to feel better . . . but not done it? We know we need more sleep, healthy food, less caffeine, more water, and to move our bodies and get our hearts pumping every day.

Instead, we do the whole revenge bedtime thing where we stay up too late after the kids have gone to bed, relishing the quiet house and no one needing us or touching us for a couple of hours. We have a glass of wine and some chocolate, and watch some TV *because we've earned it, dammit!* We slink off to bed around midnight, knowing we should have turned in earlier but not realizing that we just set ourselves up for a bad night's sleep with all of our indulgences. *Whoopsie!*

I won't get into all the cultural and psychological reasons why we do this, but what I will say is that we *must* unlearn the self-sacrificing martyr act.

I'll Rest When I'm Dead

Here's another scenario that might sound familiar: How often do you push through, working long hours and saying you'll rest later—only to get sick and end up taking some forced time off?

One of my coaching clients, I'll call her Sally, is a classic example. She came to me because she was tired of watching this play out in her own life over and over again. She knew she was overworking and pushing herself too hard, but money was tight, and she felt like she had no other choice. She was a partner in a start-up that was still in the beginning phases, and they weren't able to pay themselves a salary yet. Sally still had bills to pay, though, so in addition to her start-up duties, she was doing freelance work on the side. She was burning the candle at both ends.

Here's the thing. Sally is a smart woman, and she's been doing personal development work for a long time. She knew what she needed to do. She knew she needed to get up from her desk more, get some exercise, and restart all the healthful practices she'd dropped the moment she'd gotten so busy juggling two jobs. She also needed to set some stronger boundaries around her start-up responsibilities. But she didn't. Instead, she soldiered on. Until her body forced her to stop.

You see, every time Sally would overwork and get buried under her stress, she'd either get sick or injure herself. Her back would go out and she wouldn't be able to sit at her desk and work long hours. She'd be terribly sick and not be able to get out of bed for a couple of days. You get the idea.

It's not just Sally, though. I've seen this pattern play out dozens of times with myself, clients, and friends. Our bodies are smart—smarter than we are, sometimes—and if we refuse to take a break or slow down, eventually our bodies will make us. (Like I said, smart, and maybe just a little bit ruthless.)

And if we don't catch on and change our ways? Well, then we're destined to just keep repeating the pattern. We're like Sisyphus pushing the boulder up the hill for all eternity.

Sure, we can blame the kids for bringing germs home from school all the time, but we can't blame them for all our health woes. Neglecting our own well-being is a recipe for disaster since stress and unhealthy habits can compromise our immune systems, making us more susceptible to illness.

As wellness educator Joyce Sunada famously said, "If you don't take time for your wellness, you will be forced to take time for your illness."

Sacrificing our own needs and always putting our self-care last is a toxic habit that we must unlearn if we want to live our healthiest, happiest, most fulfilling lives. It's not selfish, it's just plain smart.

Put on your own oxygen mask, you can't pour from an empty cup, and all that good stuff. They might be clichés, but they're also true. It's time to take care of ourselves for a change. It's time to put self-care and healthy habits at the top of our to-do lists.

Chapter 6

ARE YOU A KNOWLEDGE HOARDER?

You are a smart cookie. A wise chocolate cake.
A brilliant pancake.
REY WOODMAN

My favorite character in the Harry Potter series is Hermione. Sure, she can come off as an insufferable know-it-all at times, but let's face it, the girl gets things done and saves the day more often than Harry. If it weren't for Hermione, Harry and Ron would die before their first semester at Hogwarts comes to an end. Just saying.

I appreciate intelligence and consider myself a lifelong learner. My house is full of books, and I've lost track of the number of classes I've taken over the years, well beyond my college days. I even took a certification course on neuroscience to learn brain-based coaching strategies—talk about nerdy!

Which is why it might shock those who know me well to hear me say that you don't need more titles, certifications, and another degree to change your life for the better.

Gasp! Did the nerd who said she's a lifelong learner just tell you to pause and stop acquiring more knowledge for knowledge's sake? Yes . . . kind of.

Here's the thing: Although it's amazing to keep learning and expanding our knowledge, we must be careful to not keep chasing shiny objects, looking for the new fad, and learning more and more and more but never applying what we know.

We need to apply the knowledge we already have. Sure, fill the knowledge gaps if there are some, but are you actually *using* what you know or are you just hoarding knowledge like a dragon hoards treasure?

This is a lesson I had to learn the hard way. Repeatedly.

You see, back in 2014 I heard the term *highly sensitive person* for the very first time. My oldest son was struggling, and a good friend came across the work of Elaine Aron, PhD, and sent me a link to Aron's quiz to see if my son might be a highly sensitive person (HSP). I took the quiz on his behalf and promptly burst into tears. Not because Jacob was an HSP (though he is) but because I'm an HSP too.

I didn't cry because it meant something was "wrong" with us (there isn't). I cried because it was the first time I felt like I wasn't alone in my sensitivity. Like it wasn't just a Julie problem.

Like I wasn't broken in some way and the only person who felt like this. I was part of a minority—only 20 percent of the world's population is highly sensitive—but I wasn't alone. There was a name for what I am, and it's not a disorder or some sort of affliction, either.

HSPs have sensory processing sensitivity. Basically, our nervous systems are extra sensitive. We notice more than the average person, take it all in, and deeply process the information. Because we're taking in so much all the time, we can easily get overwhelmed. It's like the dial is turned up to 11 all the time, and it can be a lot to handle.

Being able to identify myself as an HSP was life changing in many ways. Sure, I'm different, but I'm not alone in my sensitivity, and it's even an evolutionary advantage in some ways. Highly sensitive folks were keeping their tribes alive back in the caveman days by being more highly attuned to their surroundings and to others. *Yay, us, keeping everyone alive!*

My mistake, however, was not taking this newfound knowledge and learning how to leverage it and better my life. It was a big moment for me, but instead of going off and focusing on other things, I wish I'd looked for the practical application. I took on the label of HSP, but I didn't figure out how to apply the knowledge to improve my life. If I had, I might have learned about nervous system regulation techniques six years sooner than I ultimately did and saved myself a lot of unnecessary suffering.

And what did I do when I finally learned about nervous system regulation techniques in 2020? I had another paradigm-shifting moment where my life made so much more sense and I realized why all the things I'd been doing to ease my stress and anxiety over the years hadn't helped. I finally had answers, and I started telling everyone who would listen all about it. (More on this in chapter 11.)

No wonder I had a panic attack in therapy—my nervous system was dysregulated and my brain wasn't in a state to process talk therapy. No wonder I had felt so angry and anxious—I was living my life in fight-or-flight mode the majority of the time. Again, hallelujah: I had some answers!

For a smart woman, I can be slow sometimes, though, when it comes to applying knowledge to my own life. I was quick to share what I had learned, but I was slower to start taking my own advice.

You have to actually do something with the knowledge you gain to change your life. You can't just race off to learn some unrelated new thing or just share what you learned. Yes, share it, but apply the knowledge, too.

Knowledge can't change you if you don't actually do something with it. Once something moves from our brains to our bones, from theory to practice, we can use it to change our lives.

I am going to share more later about how to take what I'm teaching you out into the real world, but please, for the love of Hermione, learn from my mistakes.

Don't just learn something and think, *I know that already—moving on!* or *That's cool!* without doing anything with the knowledge. Whether it's something you need to unlearn, something you already know, or brand-new information, take it and DO SOMETHING WITH IT.

Really sit with this stuff and get it into your bones. If you really feel compelled to dig deeper into research on anything I cover here, go for it. I'm not saying stop learning. What I'm saying is that instead of going wider, we need to go deeper into topics. We need to get a little obsessed. But not just with the why and the how—we need to get obsessed with taking action and applying what we learn.

I'll say it again: Common sense isn't always common practice—but for us, it needs to be. We're all very smart here—*yay, us!* So let's put this knowledge to use and change our lives already.

TWO TRUTHS
AND A LIE

Do what you can do in joy instead of
trying to do it all in misery.

JEN SINCERO

Alrighty, let's refocus and get real about where we are, what we want, and where we're headed. In section 1, you learned that high achievement and high performance are not the same things, and you unlearned some BS about willpower, stress, and hustling. Congratulations, you just dropped a lot of unnecessary baggage—I bet you're feeling lighter already!

But knowing what not to do is only half the battle. Now it's time for a reality check and to get honest with ourselves about how we've been showing up. Let's call out our own BS stories and where we've been making excuses so we can start making better choices.

That's what this section is all about. I'll help you refocus, get real about where you are, what you want, and where you're headed. Then, in section 3, I'll dive into the "how," providing you with tangible actions to help you transform your life. So, keep reading, and I'll guide you through the entire journey.

In this section, we'll take a big-picture look at our lives and see where we might be a little out of whack and what we need to bring attention to.

And before we wrap up, we'll make sure we're asking the right questions and focusing on what really matters. Setting intentions for how we want to move forward is not just a once-a-year thing, it's an all-day-every-day thing.

We've already had some fun calling out cultural BS, so let's keep it going and dig deeper into our own. Think of it like playing the game Two Truths and a Lie, where you spot the lie among the truths being told. The lies we tell ourselves aren't always intentional denials; they can be more like coping mechanisms or wishful thinking. They can be tricky to spot, just like in the game, because they often have a ring of truth to them.

It might be a bit uncomfortable to reveal these lies, sort of like leg day at the gym, but trust me, the payoff will be worth it. Real change can come only when we're addressing fact, not fiction.

And remember, once you've grasped the "what" in this section, I'll guide you through the "how" in section 3, so you can confidently take those crucial next steps.

Chapter 7

TIME FOR A REALITY CHECK

Life is what happens to you while
you're busy making other plans.
JOHN LENNON

I was sitting in the audience at a coaching event when the speaker, a world-renowned coach, asked a question that made me feel like I'd just been punched in the gut.

The question wasn't even directed at me—or at anyone in the crowd, for that matter. It was a question he'd asked one of his coaching clients in a private session, but when he retold the story, it hit a little too close to home and knocked the breath out of me. I can't remember the exact wording, but the story went something like this.

His client, a successful entrepreneur whom I'll call Bill, was complaining about an argument with his wife and how it had gone completely sideways. Bill wasn't taking any real responsibility for his part in the argument when the coach hit him with this question. He said, "Bill, what was your intention for this discussion with your wife?"

Bill was confused and replied, "I didn't really have an intention. We just started arguing."

To which the coach said, "Well, when we started working together, you said your intention was to be the best husband possible for your wife. To show up lovingly and thoughtfully and to make her a top priority. Is how you acted during this argument a good example of how you want to show up? Is that how an amazing husband acts?"

As I sat there, I asked myself, *What kind of a wife have I been? If actions speak louder than words, what have my actions been saying about me? Can I truthfully say I'm showing up the way I want to in my marriage, or am I taking my partner of over 20 years for granted?* I didn't like the answers I came up with, and frankly, I was a little ashamed. My actions and my intentions weren't aligned, and that is a terrible feeling.

I'm guessing you can relate. Maybe not about your marriage but in some area of your life. We all have at least one area, if not multiple ones, where if we take a close look, we're not proud of what we see.

We say our family is our number one priority . . . but we work late nights and weekends, and ignore the kids when they want to play. *Just 10 more minutes, honey. Mommy has to finish this.* But 10 minutes turns into 60 minutes, and the kids give up asking.

We say our health is a top priority . . . but we're sneaking sweets when no one is looking, sitting for 10 hours a day, and getting winded taking the dog for a walk.

If we're talking the talk but not walking the walk, it's time to take a good, hard look at ourselves. But listen, this isn't about beating ourselves up or feeling ashamed—it's about getting honest about our intentions and whether they align with our actions.

Let's face it—none of us are perfect, and that's okay. But when we step back and look at how we've been showing up over the past weeks, months, or even years, are we happy with what we see? Is it in line with our values and aspirations, or are we veering off course?

If we have good intentions but fail to act accordingly, it's time to reevaluate our approach. Just remember—this is not about placing blame, but rather a moment of self-reflection. After all, if our goals aren't rooted in reality, we're going to have a tough time getting where we want to go.

Think of it like planning a road trip: If we put the wrong destination into our GPS, it doesn't matter how accurate our directions are, we'll end up in the wrong place. The same is true for our goals: If they're not grounded in reality, we won't be able to achieve them no matter how hard we try.

Take a good look at your life, have your very own Taylor Swift moment, raise your hand, and admit, "It's me, hi, I'm the problem, it's me."

You might be feeling like the anti-hero right about now if you took the time to really reflect on how you've been showing up in your life. I get it. As I said, it can feel like a punch in the gut. Rather than using the stories to beat ourselves up, what we need to do now is own them and take responsibility for writing new stories.

You had your anti-hero moment—now it's time to create your metamorphosis story.

So let's take a deep breath and commit to being honest with ourselves. Let's approach this with a sense of self-compassion and a willingness to take action in the direction of our true desires.

Chapter 8

WHO'S DRIVING? TIME TO TAKE THE WHEEL

Happiness is not something ready-made.
It comes from your own actions.
THE DALAI LAMA

et's be real here: Calling out our own BS stories can be an emotional experience. It's likely that you thought of some specific scenarios that made you cringe as you read the last chapter and reflected on how you've been showing up. But recognizing those stories is an important step, and it's crucial to remember that they don't define us as people—they just point to areas where we can improve. *Yay—we have some things to work on!*

Now, let's take a 30,000-foot view of your life so we can spot the areas where you're thriving and the ones that need attention.

The truth is, our lives are never going to be perfectly balanced all the time—and that's okay. We don't need to strive for perfection to have an amazing life. But we do want to make sure that no one area is getting too out of whack for too long, because that's when our overall quality of life starts to suffer. Sure, there may be times when work takes priority, but we need to make sure we don't get stuck in that mode to the detriment of our loved ones.

A popular way to do this overview is to take a Wheel of Life assessment. Also commonly referred to as a life wheel, this is a powerful tool because it gives you a visual representation of the way your life is currently, compared with the way you'd like it to be. It is called the Wheel of Life because each area of your life is mapped on a circle divided by spokes, like a wheel. You rate your satisfaction in each area from 1 to 10, color in that "slice of the pie," and then see how each area stacks up. It's not uncommon to have a pretty clunky-looking wheel, with some areas close to 10 and other areas only, say, a 4.

The concept was originally created by Paul J. Meyer, founder of Success Motivation Institute in the 1960s, and has been used and adapted by countless coaching programs over the years.

You can easily create your own Wheel of Life with a pen and paper or download my version at www.AFewGoodHabitsBook. com.

I recommend using the following six areas for the wheel: health, significant other, family and friends, career (or financial security), hobbies (or creative life), and spiritual life (or personal growth).

Don't get too hung up on the specific naming of each category. The idea is just to take a look at the important areas of your life, rate how you're feeling about each area, and see where you might be out of balance.

For example, on a scale of 1 to 10, where would you rank if I asked, "Do you have the mental and physical energy needed to meet life's challenges and rise to the opportunities presented to you?" Would you be a 1 because that's not at all true, a 10 because that describes you perfectly, or somewhere in between?

What if I asked about your mission and how you're contributing to the world with your work? On a scale of 1 to 10, how strongly do you feel that your work adds value to the world and that you are showing up as your best self in your career?

Take a moment to ask yourself these types of questions for each of the six areas. Where do you score high and where is your wheel looking a little deflated?

Now that you have your scores, bring your priorities to mind. What really matters to you? There's no right or wrong answer, but what matters to you? Really? Not what do you *think* you *should* be doing, but what do you really care about?

When one of my clients, Shannon, did this assessment, the area of hobbies was a 1 for her. Now, a score that low might have raised a big red flag, but she was an 8 or 10 in every other area except for health, which was a 5, so overall she was doing very well. When we discussed her results, it was clear that her health being a 5 was an area of concern and something she needs a plan to improve, yet scoring a 1 for hobbies wasn't nearly as much of a problem. Why?

It all comes down to priorities, and her health was at the top of the list. Also, Shannon's work is fulfilling her need for creativity, so although she doesn't have a hobby per se, that need is being met. In fact, if we look at the area of hobbies as her overall creative life instead, her score improves dramatically.

We also explored how she can view the lifestyle changes she's making to improve her health as hobbies, so that they feel more fun and enjoyable.

For example, she could see cooking healthy meals as a chore and one more thing to juggle, or as a hobby she can enjoy with her family. That might look like taking cooking classes with her husband or teaching her daughter how to cook and educating her about making healthy food choices.

Likewise, exercise could feel like another to-do on her already long list of daily activities, or she can look for ways to make it fun. In Shannon's case, we discovered that incorporating new hobbies could not only help her reach her health goals but also bring her more joy and fulfillment.

Running isn't her thing and doesn't have to be. Maybe she'll learn how to Hula-Hoop, or join a spin class with amazing music and a fun instructor to keep her motivated. A great question to ask here is *How can I make improving this area of my life more fun and enjoyable?*

So, if you scored low in any given area, ask yourself two questions:

1. *Is this area a neglected priority that really does need some attention to raise my score?*

2. *Is this area of life low on my priority list right now for a reason? Why?*

Aim for an 8 to 10 in each area, but know that at different times, you'll score some areas higher than others and that's okay. Approach this assessment with an open mind and a sense of curiosity. Rather than dismissing an area that doesn't rank high, see if you can find ways to incorporate it that align with your values and goals. Who knows—you might discover new sources of joy and growth you didn't even know existed!

Don't Make This Mistake!

Here's something to keep in mind: A lot of people make the mistake of doing this assessment at the start of the year and then forgetting about it. This shouldn't be a one-and-done exercise. Taking a big-picture look in January is great, but it's important to make this a regular habit—whether that's monthly or quarterly.

Why? Because our priorities and values are constantly evolving, and we need to adapt accordingly. Although it's normal for some areas of life to be high while others are low, we don't want to neglect any given area for too long—and certainly not forever.

That's why I recommend doing this assessment at least quarterly and taking a good hard look at any areas that you consistently score lower than 8. Ask yourself why they're a low priority and what actions you can take to improve them. On the flip side, for areas you ranked an 8 or above, ask yourself how you can maintain that momentum and even apply what's working well to areas that need improvement.

Remember, our lives are constantly in motion, and it's up to us to keep up with the changes and make the most of each day. By making this assessment a regular practice, we can ensure we never stray too far off the path for too long.

Chapter 9

STOP DOING THE DECISION HOKEYPOKEY

I'm as proud of many of the things we haven't
done as the things we have done.
STEVE JOBS

If you've taken the time to reflect and call out your BS stories as well as do a big-picture assessment of your life, you should have a good idea now of the general life areas that need more of your time and attention.

Your next step is deciding what success looks like to you in each area you want to improve. For example, if you want to make your health a top priority, what does that look like exactly? How will you know when you've reached your goals? You need to begin with the end in mind or you'll just end up taking a whole lot of action that leads nowhere.

Book writing is a perfect example of why this type of planning is important. When I hired a coach to help me through the book writing and publishing process, one of the first things she told me was that we needed to nail down the goal of the book and the journey I wanted to take people on. Getting really clear on the vision for the book as well as the outline was critical to set myself up for success. There's a whole lot of information that I *could* write about, but just because I can doesn't mean I should. If it doesn't support the goal of the book, it doesn't belong here.

My coach, Lanette Pottle, told me that it's not uncommon for aspiring authors to be told to just sit down and write, but that's actually terrible advice. Without a clear vision and structure, many people end up working on their book for literally years and never finish. They put a ton of time and effort in, but all of that work never results in a finished product. Why? They didn't have a clear enough vision. They didn't have a structure, or an outline to follow, so instead, they took a whole lot of action that led nowhere.

Whether you're writing a book, optimizing your health, or growing your business, you need to know where you're headed and the key activities that will help get you where you want to be.

Needle Movers

Once you know your end goal, you need to discover the needle-moving activities that will get you results. The good news is, you don't need to reinvent the wheel. Success leaves clues. You're not the first person to ever write a book, lose weight, or start a business. You don't have to start from scratch and figure everything out yourself.

What did others before you do to get the outcomes you're after? In almost every pursuit there are generally a handful of key activities that lead to positive outcomes. The answer isn't just to take more and more action, but rather to take the right actions. Your job is to learn the handful of key activities that will put you on the path to success.

Remember, no matter the goal you're after, answers are out there. Find a book, mentor, coach, or course on the topic and get help. Regardless of your budget, you have options. In fact, there are so many options, you might feel overwhelmed when trying to decide which route to take.

Probability Storms

Once you know the result you're after and what you're striving for, how do you decide which route to take to improve your life? There are so many options, and so many paths forward. This is where a lot of us fail to set ourselves up for success.

The day before I sat down to write this chapter, my family and I went to the movie theater to see *Ant-Man and the Wasp: Quantumania,* and I was provided the perfect analogy for just how overwhelming it can be when it feels like we have too many options. Too many possible paths forward.

In the movie is a scene where Ant-Man, Scott Lang, finds himself in a "probability storm" in the quantum realm. In this probability storm, all possible versions of Scott exist at the same time.

That means that every time Scott makes even a small decision, a new Ant-Man pops up. He takes a step forward with his left foot, and an infinite number of "new" Scotts appear—one who steps with the right foot instead, another who stands still, another who takes a step back, and so on.

Very quickly, a million different Ant-Men are causing a whole lot of chaos instead of getting Scott closer to his ultimate goal. He's literally holding himself back and about to be overcome by all the possibilities when he finally starts making progress.

How? He remembers that every version of him wants the same thing: They all want to save his daughter, Cassie, and that's all that matters.

Although it's unlikely we'll ever find ourselves stuck in the quantum realm like Ant-Man, similarly frustrating moments play out in our lives all the time.

You decide you want to lose weight and make your health a priority only to find yourself lost down a rabbit hole of choices . . .

Should you do keto, paleo, or the Mediterranean diet?

Yes or no to intermittent fasting?

Several small meals a day or just three bigger ones?

Should you work out in the morning or evening?

Cardio or strength training?

Group classes, solo, or with a trainer?

Just like Ant-Man, you're suddenly buried under what feels like an infinite number of choices. It's easy to get overwhelmed and do nothing at this point. It's also easy to pick something, only to constantly second-guess yourself and therefore be only half committed to your path. One foot in and one foot out. You're doing the decision hokeypokey, and it is setting you up for failure.

Michael Jordan once said, "Once I made a decision, I never thought about it again." That's the attitude you want. No FOMO. No questioning your own judgment. There's no perfect option. Just choose, commit fully, and start moving toward your goal confidently. *But is it really that simple?*

Planning for Failure Sets You Up to Succeed

You're fully committed, you're taking action, and you're trying your damnedest to not second-guess yourself . . . but you're also human.

So although the goal is no second-guessing, I also want to pause here and be real for a moment. Those "Just Do It" declarations may sound cool when Nike says them, and they're certainly common in many self-improvement books, but part of my job is to call out BS. And telling you to just commit and do the thing and not look back is setting you up to use willpower to white-knuckle your way through the hard times. We already know that doesn't work. So what do we do?

Well, we admit that we're human and recognize there will come a time when we question ourselves. We also admit that there may come a time when we really do need to change course. We're committed to the outcome, but we don't want to get overly attached to how we get there.

There's a fine line we need to walk here. How do we commit fully to a choice but also leave the door open to trying something new if this path isn't working? How do we know when it's time to pivot or even quit? How do we keep from getting sucked back into the probability storm or doing the decision hokeypokey?

The answer is to plan for "failure" so you know how to handle it.

Know exactly what you will do if you veer off course. Decide in advance what failure looks like, what temptation looks like, when to quit, and how to handle common obstacles.

I know this goes contrary to a lot of advice out there that tells you to focus only on the positive, lest you manifest an outcome you don't want. I'll be blunt: That's like saying having a spare tire in the trunk is a bad idea because it might make you "manifest" a flat tire. It's a logical fallacy, and we're not playing that game.

This isn't about obsessing about all the ways you could possibly fail and giving up. This is about preparing for real-life scenarios, for inevitable challenges (like flat tires, rain on your running days, and birthday cake in the break room). When you know in advance what you'll do when challenges arise, you free up your mind from constantly second-guessing.

Rather than constantly questioning whether something is working and what you should do, it's helpful to create a set of guidelines you can refer to. That way, you don't have to reinvent the wheel every time you face a challenge. You don't need to rely on your strength during moments of weakness—you just need to follow your plan.

By creating "if-then" plans, you're better equipped to handle obstacles that may arise. You've already decided how to approach difficult situations, which makes it easier to stay on track and avoid getting derailed.

Let's use weight loss and dieting as an example. You've chosen to follow a keto diet plan to lose weight.

Under what circumstances would you decide to give up on keto and try a different diet plan? Would it be based on how you feel? How much weight you've lost in a certain amount of time or something else? What does "failure" on the diet look like? If you don't know, you won't know when to try something new or keep going.

And then there are all the temptations that come up when you're trying to lose weight. What do you do if you walk into the kitchen and want a cookie? What do you do if someone in your office has a birthday and there's cake in the break room? What do you do if you were planning to run this morning but it's snowing and icy out?

If you don't plan in advance, odds are that you're going to make a choice that doesn't support your goals more often than you'd like. Your willpower will fail you. If you already know your "if-then" answers to these challenges, you don't have to rely on willpower; you just have to use the answer you already came up with. Over time, the responses become automatic, and you don't have to waste time debating your options. The decision is already made for you.

- *If I walk into the kitchen and see a cookie I want, then I'll have a big glass of water instead.*

- *If I get up and the weather is too bad to run, then I will get on the treadmill instead.*

- *If there's cake in the break room, then I'll have one of the low-calorie treats in my desk instead.*

Think of it this way: If someone were to offer me a cigarette, I wouldn't have to think about it. I decided a long time ago that I will never smoke. The decision is already made. I don't have to waste time debating it.

How can you make the decisions in your life that cut and dried, that automatic?

Patience, Grasshopper

Now that you've determined what success looks like and have a plan, I want to leave you with one last reminder in regard to taking action, and that is to bring a whole load of patience with you on your journey.

Be honest: How many times have you set out to reach a goal, only to get impatient when results weren't coming fast enough?

I have certainly been guilty of this. I have dieted for a week and been furious that I didn't lose at least five pounds. I've exercised for two weeks only to be supremely ticked that not only was I still struggling and huffing my way through workouts, but I also wasn't feeling the workout high that people talk about. *Where's my dopamine, dammit? I thought working out was supposed to make you feel good. I don't feel good. I'm sore and tired and clearly pretty grumpy still!*

Even though I know that weight loss takes time and I didn't get this muffin top overnight and shouldn't expect to lose it overnight, it's easy to lose sight of sometimes—especially when you're hangry.

So if you struggle with patience when it comes to getting results too, I get it, trust me.

When I'm struggling with patience, I remind myself that sometimes even the best stories start out slow, only to get really juicy in the fifth chapter.

I mean, how many times have you started a TV series and thought, *This kinda sucks*, but because everyone you know has been raving about it, you stick with it? You know the good part is coming.

Case in point: I was late to the party when it came to watching *Schitt's Creek*. People kept raving about it, but when I finally watched the first episode, I was underwhelmed. I mean, it was okay, but I wasn't hooked by any means. It took a few episodes to get great. Then it got amazing.

I'm glad I pushed through the less-than-stellar start; otherwise, I would have missed out on everything from "Fold in the cheese!" to Patrick's rendition of "Simply the Best" and every one of David's hilarious facial expressions and snarky remarks. I would have missed all the good stuff.

Life is just like that sometimes. Sometimes we have to get past the *meh* to make it to the amazing. Keep going. Be patient. Stick to your plan.

Chapter 10

YOUR "WHY" ISN'T ENOUGH

Motivation is what gets you started.
Habit is what keeps you going.
JIM ROHN

What if knowing your "why" isn't enough? What if it's not the key to success after all?

That's the question I started asking myself not that long ago, and I have to admit it felt almost blasphemous to consider.

After all, if you've done any sort of personal growth work, you've surely been told, like me, that the key to making your dreams come true and achieving your goals is knowing your "why"—your purpose and vision for the future and why it matters to you. The rationale is that your why will keep you focused and motivated when things get hard.

On the surface it makes sense. It's hard to argue against because it seems very logical. I've also seen research on high performers that says that one of the keys to their success is that they have a high sense of necessity to succeed. Success is not just a "nice to have"—they feel they "must" do a good job. They must bring their A-game. Again, this made sense to me.

Yet, despite having done countless purpose exercises over the years—on my own and with others coaching me through them—the hard truth was that my why had rarely seen me through hard times and to the finish line for challenging goals.

I knew this, and yet it's what everyone says to do, so I kept doing the exercises and even leading some of my own coaching clients through purpose work as well. I believed that it "should" work and that if it didn't, it was just some sort of personal failing of mine. It wasn't until recently that I dared to deeply question the validity of the method.

I'll be completely honest and admit that I didn't start to seriously question the concept until I started writing this book. My original intent was for this chapter to be about purpose work and finding your why. I was going to pass on what I'd learned over the years like a good little student.

I even knew the story I wanted to share about how your why can motivate you to make changes—the story of finding out that my son Josh has attention-deficit hyperactivity disorder, or ADHD.

You see, the ADHD diagnosis came as a surprise because I knew very little about all the ways that ADHD can manifest. I dove into the research to get a better understanding, and one of the first things I learned is that neurodivergent kids need their parents to be calm and well regulated.

By that point, I was already studying nervous system regulation and understood the concept of co-regulation. The idea is that you can essentially share your calm with someone and help ground them. Alternatively, your chaotic energy can feed off someone else and cause more problems. But remember, there was a period of time when I was accumulating knowledge but not applying it to my life in serious ways. I was sort of dabbling with the knowledge when it came to making real-life changes.

Josh's diagnosis was a slap in the face and motivated me to do my own work. My own physical and emotional well-being had never been so clearly linked to my child's well-being, and it got my attention. It became my why and it motivated me . . . for a while.

The embarrassing truth I've never shared before is that that motivation lasted only so long. It got me into action, but it didn't sustain the work long term. I eventually became inconsistent with my exercises, and once again, I blamed myself. *What's wrong with me that even my son needing me well regulated isn't enough to keep me motivated day in and day out?* I thought. *I must be a terrible mother.*

It wasn't the first time my why had failed me, though. I had used my kids as motivation before when coaches asked me why I wanted to focus on my health. "I want to be able to play with them and be active in the evenings instead of crashing in front of the TV," I'd say.

I've also pointed to my extended family's less-than-stellar health and used that as my why over the years. Name a health condition, and someone in my family has probably had it. I know all of my risk factors, and I want to live not only a long life but a healthy, active one. All fantastic reasons that *should* be motivating, right?

Then why couldn't I stay motivated for more than a few weeks or months at best? Why couldn't I stop eating the Thin Mints? Why has my weight yo-yoed over the years? Why wasn't my why strong enough?

Here's the thing. I think it's a safe bet that I'm not the only one who has struggled with this. You probably have as well, if not with diet and exercise, then in other areas of your life. I didn't think this was just a "Julie problem," so if I was going to call BS on all the things we've been taught that don't work in the real world, I had to take a closer look at purpose work as well, no matter how blasphemous it felt.

If focusing on my why wasn't working—why not? Was it truly just a personal shortcoming, or was it something else?

I believe the answer lies in the fact that much like willpower, motivation doesn't really work. And what is our why if not motivation to keep going and working toward our goals? We're looking for the thing that will sustain us and motivate us. In other words, our why—our purpose and motivation.

Your Why Is Your Motivation . . . But Motivation Doesn't Work

I recently came across a piece of research that made it all click and confirmed why I'd been struggling.

In 2001, researchers in Great Britain began working with 248 people to build better exercise habits over the course of two weeks.[7] The subjects were divided into three groups.

The first group was the control group. They were simply asked to track how often they exercised.

The second group was the "motivation" group. They were asked to not only track their workouts but also to read some material on the benefits of exercise. The researchers also explained to the group how exercise could reduce the risk of coronary heart disease and improve heart health.

Finally, there was the third group. These subjects received the same presentation as the second group, ensuring that they had equal levels of motivation. However, they were also asked to formulate a plan for when and where they would exercise over the following week. Specifically, each member of the third group completed the following sentence: "During the next week, I will partake in at least 20 minutes of vigorous exercise on [day] at [time] in [place]."

After receiving these instructions, all three groups left.

In both the control group and the motivation group, only 35 to 38 percent of people exercised at least once per week. The motivational presentation had zero impact on behavior. They knew why they should exercise, but they still didn't take action.

However, in the group where the members made a plan, 91 percent of them exercised at least once per week—more than double the other groups' rate.

The simple act of writing down a plan that said exactly when and where they planned to exercise made participants in Group 3 much more likely to actually follow through.

Perhaps even more surprising than how well having a plan worked was the fact that motivation didn't work at all. The researchers said, "Motivation . . . had no significant effects on exercise behavior."[8]

This study illuminated the issue I've always had with relying on a why to see me through. Motivation and a basic desire for change (a why) don't get results—having a clear plan of action is the key differentiator.

And yet, when most people set out to achieve their goals, they rely on motivation and willpower to make changes. They're told that if their why is strong enough, it will motivate them to see their goals to completion. It's time to call BS on this belief!

Implementation Intentions

The sentence that the third group filled out is what researchers refer to as an implementation intention, which is a plan you make about when and where to act.[9] That is, how you intend to implement a particular habit.

Hundreds of studies have shown that implementation intentions are effective for sticking to our goals, and they increase the odds that people will maintain habits as varied as recycling, voting, studying, going to sleep early, and stopping smoking.[10]

Implementation intentions are what we need to make our goals a reality. Not just motivation, or willpower, and not just a lofty purpose and why. We need a clear plan that sets us up for success.

In section 3, I explain exactly how to create implementation intentions to reach your goals and stick to your new habits.

Does This Mean Your "Why" Doesn't Matter?

After realizing that motivation, aka your why, isn't the key to success, my next question was Does that mean your why doesn't matter at all? Is it irrelevant?

No, I don't believe it's irrelevant; I think we just need to think of our why in a different light. Although I don't believe motivation or willpower work when it comes to seeing our goals to completion, I still use purpose work in an important way—as part of identity work.

James Clear, author of *Atomic Habits*, advocates for creating "identity-based habits" by focusing on who we wish to become, not what we want to achieve.

Clear writes, "Anyone can convince themselves to visit the gym or eat healthy once or twice, but if you don't shift the belief behind the behavior, then it is hard to stick with long-term changes. Improvements are only temporary until they become part of who you are. It's one thing to say I'm the type of person who *wants* this. It's something very different to say I'm the type of person who *is* this."[11]

So when I think about my purpose, I ask myself, *What type of person could get the outcome I want?*

For example, what would a healthy person do? What would a productive person do? These questions help reveal the identity I want to work toward and the habits that support that identity.

It's often said that knowing your purpose and values is important because it gives you a guiding light to keep you on the right track. They act as your North Star. That sounds good, and I don't know about you, but I've never been great at navigation.

If you gave me directions to head north out of my neighborhood, I'd look at you like you had three heads and ask if that was left, right, or straight ahead. *North* wouldn't mean much to me in practice, and neither do the lofty ideals of purpose and values. I don't really know how to use them to navigate. They're just not concrete enough.

Knowing the identity I want to embody, on the other hand, helps me determine the habits to focus on so I can take action.

We'll discuss how to leverage identity-based habits and other practical tactics in the next section.

FOUR HABITS
TO RULE THEM ALL

Success is a few good habits repeated
every day. Failure is a few bad decisions
repeated every day.

JIM ROHN

After reading countless books and research studies on behavior change, habits, willpower, and goal setting over the years, I've realized that a few key concepts hold true across all the research. These are ideas and strategies that everyone seems to agree on—the kind of advice that cuts through the noise of all the so-called experts bombarding us with information.

My goal in this section is to bring together the best of the best from all the research I've read and make it simple for you to apply in your own life. I'll share my journey of sifting through countless ideas and finally finding the gems that genuinely made a difference for me and can do the same for you.

Five core truths emerged from all the research:

1. Real transformation takes place at the identity level.

2. Success lies in starting small and keeping things simple.

3. Planning is essential for success, and plans must be specific and account for potential failures.

4. Motivation and willpower are not reliable—you have to create an environment that sets you up for success.

5. It takes only a few good habits to change your life—the trick is selecting the right habits to focus on.

In this section, we'll put these five truths into action to help you create habits that stick. By understanding that real change starts with how you see yourself, and that taking small steps and planning for obstacles is key, you'll be on your way to creating habits that last.

We'll also talk about how to create an environment that supports your new habits, rather than relying solely on motivation and willpower. And the best part? You don't need to overhaul your entire life—just a few good habits can make a big difference.

Together, we'll explore the what, the why, and the how in the chapters that follow: what habits to focus on, why I chose them and why they make such a difference, and how to actually follow through to make meaningful changes instead of giving up the first time it gets hard.

As we explore these ideas, I'll be sharing both scientific research and my own experiences. It's important to know there's science to back up these strategies, but I also want to keep it real and show you how they have worked in my life.

If you were playing along in section 2 and getting clarity on where you are now and where you're headed, you probably have some big-picture goals in mind. Regardless of what you're working on, the good news is that the habits you're about to learn will help build a solid foundation to support all of your goals. When you're operating from a strong baseline of health and vitality, everything gets easier. That's the beauty of a few good habits.

So, let's dive in and learn how to apply these core truths to create the four high-impact habits that will help you achieve your goals!

Chapter 11

THE FANTASTIC FOUR: YOUR LIFE-CHANGING HABITS

Considering that our habits create our life, there is arguably no single skill that is more important for you to learn and master than controlling your habits.
HAL ELROD

Before diving into the nitty-gritty details of the "fantastic four," I want to explain their significance and why I've selected these particular habits as the focus of this book.

But first, I've got a confession to make. I'm obviously a total habit nerd. For years, I've read books by all the experts—James Clear, Charles Duhigg, Kelly McGonigal, Brendon Burchard—and soaked up everything they had to say. Although their works were informative and full of valuable advice, I had one critical issue: I wasn't taking action on what I learned, at least not consistently over the long term.

What gives? I thought. *Am I just a weirdo who likes to read but doesn't take action—or is something else going on here?*

The problem, I finally realized, was that I wasn't sure where to start. I had learned a lot about habits, but I wasn't sure which habits I should focus on. All the experts seemed to agree that exercise was crucial, but beyond that, I was stumped and overwhelmed.

The Power of Keystone Habits

Charles Duhigg's work introduced me to the concept of keystone habits, small changes that unintentionally carry over into other aspects of our lives, sparking "chain reactions that help other good habits take hold."[12] These high-impact habits create a ripple effect that improves numerous aspects of your life.

Duhigg points to exercise as a perfect keystone habit, saying, "Typically, people who exercise start eating better and becoming more productive at work. They smoke less and show more patience with colleagues and family. They use their credit cards less frequently and say they feel less stressed. . . . [E]xercise is a keystone habit that triggers widespread change."[13]

It's like a domino effect, but instead of tumbling into a pile, everything falls neatly into place when you tap into a keystone habit. Duhigg isn't the only habit expert extolling the benefits of keystone habits either—they are clearly a key to success.

Duhigg even goes as far as saying that anything can become a keystone habit if it has the power to make you see yourself in a different way.

That sounds great and all, but it's also overwhelming to contemplate. *Anything can become a keystone habit? Anything?* I didn't know what to do with that revelation.

No More Guesswork, No More Uncertainty

It wasn't enough to know about keystone habits in broad terms. I needed a clear path to follow, a well-defined set of habits to focus on, and the right guidance to ensure success. My earlier attempts to implement the advice from these books had been unfocused and overwhelming, leading to limited progress.

That's why I decided to write this book. I don't want you to encounter the same challenges. I don't want to just give you broad advice and leave you to find the best keystone habits on your own.

Instead, I've distilled the wisdom of these experts to handpick four keystone habits that I believe will create a massive ripple effect in your life. No more guesswork, no more uncertainty—I provide a clear roadmap to guide you through the process of building them.

The Fantastic Four

The four high-impact habits that have the power to transform your life are

1. sleep routines,

2. regular exercise and movement,

3. intentionally planning your days, and

4. mindfulness and meditation.

In the upcoming chapters, I delve deeply into the many benefits of each habit, but for now, I want to highlight my primary reason for selecting them: Not only are they keystone habits, but they are extremely effective at reducing stress levels.

I'm sure you've noticed from my personal stories that I've struggled with stress and anxiety throughout my life. I bet you've encountered similar challenges, especially with the high-stress environment we're living in globally.

I believe it's crucial to prioritize habits that help us reduce stress and improve our health and well-being. And that's what sets these habits apart—they provide effective ways to manage stress and promote overall wellness.

These four keystone habits will have far-reaching ripple effects on your mental, emotional, and physical health, as well as your productivity and success. *Talk about bang for your buck!*

How to Have a Not-So-Nervous System

Back in chapter 4, we discussed the "upside" of stress and how to use it to your advantage. And although I no longer think of stress as the enemy, it is something we need to better manage.

Remember, the goal isn't a stress-free life; the goal is to live a meaningful life and learn tools to help you handle the stress

that will inevitably come up along the way. These high-impact habits are the tools that can help you manage that stress.

Nervous system regulation techniques play a key role in reducing our stress. I've hinted at the importance of nervous system regulation before, but let me take a moment to explain the role it plays in stress.

Stress is a sympathetic nervous system response. To put it in the simplest terms possible, stress lives in the body first. Honestly, I was shocked to learn that, because I had always thought of stress mainly as a mental process.

Sure, I knew I had physical signs and symptoms of stress—a racing heart, sweaty palms, stomachaches, headaches, tense muscles, teeth grinding, and even an eye twitch. Heck, I was a walking, talking example of how stress shows up in your body! And yet I still thought of stress as a mental process, probably because I tend to get so caught up in my thoughts. The anxious thoughts spiraling around in my head all day every day were how I defined stress—I thought of the physical symptoms as nothing more than side effects.

Worrisome thoughts are only half the stress story, and we can't just think our way out of stress, which is what I spent most of my life trying to do—especially once I started learning about mindset work. I thought I just needed to focus on the positive, think better thoughts, and use grit and determination to calm myself down and stop worrying so much.

It's no wonder that didn't work—I was completely ignoring my body's role in the stress response. The more I chided myself for worrying and told myself to calm down, the worse I felt. I'd worry about worrying so much, certain I was going to give myself a heart attack someday . . . and then I'd worry about that!

How Stress Shows Up in Our Bodies

To put it simply, when we sense a threat or the stakes feel very high in a situation, our sympathetic nervous system launches into a fight-or-flight response. Everyone is familiar with this idea—it is the evolutionary response that kept our ancestors alive by sending our bodies into high gear so we can throw a punch or run like hell when facing a threat.

Fortunately, as we discussed in chapter 4, fight-or-flight is not the only option we have, *but* if that's been our go-to response for decades, it's pretty ingrained by now. Not to mention the fact that fight-or-flight sometimes serves us and isn't a response we're trying to eliminate entirely.

The goal instead is twofold: First, we want to make our nervous system less overreactive so we don't launch into fight-or-flight over every little thing. Second, we need to start chipping away at the backlog of stress we've accrued over the years.

That's right—a backlog of stress. You see, if we don't deal with our stress, it doesn't just go away. When people experience chronic or repeated stress, they can get stuck in fight-or-flight mode. Our body holds on to stress like a hoarder holds on to junk, and the stress just keeps piling up until we do something about it.

Stress Debt

The way I like to explain this backlog of stress is with a concept I call stress debt. Stress debt is how I describe the accumulation of stress over time, similar to the concept of sleep debt.

I'm sure you're familiar with sleep debt: When you don't get enough sleep over a series of days, the negative effects start to compound, and your brain and body functioning deteriorates.

The same is true for stress. When you experience stress for an extended period, it begins to accumulate, and the effects can be just as harmful as sleep debt.

To understand stress debt, let's pretend that every day you accrue "10 units" of stress. The causes of your stress will vary every day—maybe one day you get a flat tire, another you get a call from school that your child is sick, and another day it's just a lot of little stressors that all add up.

Regardless of what causes your stress, imagine that at the end of today, you go to bed with 10 units of stress. Fortunately, you get a restful eight hours of sleep tonight and knock off seven stress units. *Hurray!*

However, that means when you wake up tomorrow morning, you still have three units of stress. The good night's sleep wasn't quite enough to wipe out all 10 units. This wouldn't be too big of a deal, but because you have another "typical" day, you accrue another 10 units of stress, so tomorrow when you go to bed, you will have 13 units to sleep off. Even if you get another great night's sleep, you wake up the next day with six units of stress.

You can see how the stress can really build up over time if this is how your typical day plays out. If you're not very intentional about setting your balance back to zero every day, you will quickly have a huge backlog of stress to chip away at.

Getting adequate sleep is going to go a long way toward reducing your daily stress debt, so that's key, but you need other tactics as well to get you to zero and work on that backlog you've been growing over the years.

One key way we can do this is with exercise, which signals to the vagus nerve that we're safe and can relax. The vagus nerve serves as an on/off switch of sorts for the fight-or-flight response and can help us return to a calmer, more regulated state, so we want to do everything we can to strengthen it.

If you'd like to geek out on the exact science of how this all works, look into the work of Stephen Porges and his Polyvagal Theory. My goal here isn't to give you an in-depth scientific explanation of the nervous system, just a basic view of what is happening in your body when you get stressed.

The big takeaway I want you to focus on is this: Stress is not just a mental process. Stress is very much a physical response that hijacks our brains and our bodies.

Stress is like a wildfire. It may start small, but it can quickly spread and consume everything in its path. And just like a wildfire, stress doesn't discriminate—it affects every part of our body. Our heart rate increases, our muscles tense up, and our breathing becomes shallow. Our amygdala, the "threat center" of our brain, even redirects blood flow away from our prefrontal cortex, the logical, decision-making part of our brain. Our bodies are flooded with stress hormones like cortisol and adrenaline, and even our digestion is affected.

Just like firefighters need to use all of their resources to put out a wildfire, we need to use our whole body to combat stress and prevent it from taking over our lives so we're not constantly in firefighting mode.

If you're feeling bankrupt in the stress department right about now, don't worry—that's what the habits you're about to learn are for! They will help you elevate the baseline state that you operate from every day. With more in the tank energetically, you'll be better positioned to pursue your goals.

These habits will signal to your body that you're safe, chip away at your stress debt, and give you the mental space you need to focus, make better choices, and live in a healthier, calmer, more regulated state instead of feeling like you want to punch someone, run away from your problems, or crash on the couch to recover every evening.

Chapter 12

SLEEP YOUR WAY TO THE TOP (WAIT, NOT LIKE THAT!)

It's not a trade-off between success and sleep. Science
shows that sleep is a performance-enhancement tool.
ARIANNA HUFFINGTON

What if I told you that researchers have found a "magical cure" that improves memory, increases people's ability to concentrate, strengthens the immune system, *and* decreases people's risk of being killed in accidents?

Sound too good to be true? Well, it gets even better! The treatment is completely free and has no side effects. Plus, it's enjoyable! Would you try it?

Well, get excited, because this miraculous treatment is available *today*! For most people, this "magical cure" consists of getting an extra 60–90 minutes of sleep each night. I know, it's not super sexy as far as magic pills go, but getting eight or more hours of sleep per night really is *that* good for you.

Psychologists and psychiatrists have been arguing for years that one of the most significant and overlooked public health problems in the United States is that most Americans are chronically sleep deprived. We rarely get the sleep our bodies need even though it has been proved again and again that the consequences of not getting enough sleep can be disastrous.

If you're getting less than eight hours of sleep, then listen up! Skipping out on shut-eye can lead to all sorts of problems. For one, you're putting yourself at a higher risk of getting into a car crash or performing poorly at work. Your memory, concentration, decision-making skills, and even your willpower all take a hit. And let's not forget about the toll it takes on your mood and relationships.

But wait, there's more! Lack of sleep also affects your immune system, making it more vulnerable to sickness. Plus, it's associated with a whole host of health issues like high blood pressure, heart disease, stroke, diabetes, obesity, and depression. People who chronically fail to get enough sleep may literally be cutting their lives short.[14]

When it comes to getting enough sleep, everyone seems to think they're the exception to the rule, but research consistently shows that only a tiny fraction of people can function well on fewer than eight hours of sleep each night. Although I think you're pretty special, let's assume you're not that one-in-a-million person who can function on six or fewer hours of sleep and set seven hours of sleep as your bare minimum and eight to nine hours of sleep as the gold standard.

Drunk, Sleepy . . . Same Difference!

While we're at it, let's talk about "functioning" on too little sleep. If you're reading this book, you probably don't want to just "get by" and be able to function. You want to reach higher levels of performance and be at your best, right?

Well, if you're not getting at least seven hours of sleep, consider this: You might as well be going to work drunk. Seriously.

In an extensive sleep study,[15] researchers found that it took about 18 hours of waking to reach cognitive impairments as severe as significant intoxication (0.1 percent, which is legally drunk in most places). That's the equivalent of waking up at 6 a.m. and staying up until midnight, which many people frequently do.

Basically, all-nighters and chronic sleep debt are as bad for your brainpower as downing a few beers before you start your day, but without the fun of a night out. I don't know about you, but I don't want to go through my days feeling that way.

As sleep deprivation continues over time, attention, memory, and other cognitive functions suffer. Consistently failing to get enough sleep is the biological equivalent of consistently spending more money than you make, which is why it's commonly referred to as sleep debt.

Creating Better Sleep Habits

Ideally, you're convinced at this point that getting over seven hours of sleep every night needs to become a top priority if you want to be at your best each day.

I do want to pause and recognize, however, that you might not be getting a good night's sleep for a lot of reasons. Factors like health issues, snoring (either you or a partner), sleep apnea, your menstrual cycle, menopause, or children interrupting your sleep could all be contributing to your sleep debt.

My kids were both terrible sleepers, and a five-year age gap between them meant I had a solid decade of interrupted sleep, so if you have kids keeping you up at night, I feel for you, truly. It used to drive me crazy to read advice telling me to get more sleep when my kids were little because it felt impossible at the time. I also know that if you have certain health conditions, getting a perfect's night sleep might be nearly impossible.

That is all very real and valid, and I get it if this advice puts you a bit on the defensive. I also believe that most of us are not doing everything within our power to optimize our sleep habits. That's what I focus on here: what we can improve that is within our control. Fortunately, that's quite a bit.

"Get more sleep" isn't a habit. Habits are routines that are practiced regularly, so it's really the routines that directly impact our sleep quantity and quality that we need to concentrate on here. When you get your routines down, better sleep tends to follow.

Bedtime Routines

If you have kids, you know the importance of a good bedtime routine. A routine provides a structure and predictability that allows kids to start winding down and fall asleep faster. Here's the thing: I don't believe we ever really "outgrow" the need for a good bedtime routine. Think of yourself like an overgrown toddler if it helps, and create a bedtime routine that will bring some order to your life in the hours leading up to bed. Do order and predictability sound boring? *Good. A little boredom might help you sleep, you rebel!*

Setting up your routine starts with doing some basic math. Most of us have a set wake-up time, thanks to our schedules and our kids' schedules. What time do you need to be in bed, lights out, to get eight hours of sleep? If you know it takes you 30 minutes to fall asleep every night, factor that in and get to bed 8.5 hours before your alarm goes off.

Now work backward from there to set a few more benchmarks for yourself. How long does it take you to get ready for bed? What do you do every night, and how long does it all take? If it takes you an hour to prep lunches for the next day, let the dogs out, wash your face and brush your teeth, and so on, then set an alarm for one hour before your lights-out time so you don't forget to start putting everything into motion on time.

I have no shame in the fact that I rely heavily on alarms for everything from waking up to picking up the kids to heading to bed every night. Knowing that I have an alarm set reduces my stress and mental load. It takes only a minute to set up alarms on your phone, so take advantage of this super-easy way to meet your goals.

I know this is all super basic—but are you doing it? Or do you look up from a screen every night and realize it suddenly got very late, like it's some sort of a surprise?

Your Sleep Environment

Speaking of screens—smartphones, computers, tablets, and TVs all emit blue light that disrupts our natural sleep cycles. Decreasing exposure to light in the evening, and blue light in particular, is an easy way to help your body prepare for sleep.

Why? Research has revealed that light is a powerful factor in aligning our daily routines and has a major impact on our body's internal clock, or circadian rhythm.[16]

Ban TV from the bedroom and turn off all of your devices one to two hours before bed. If you absolutely can't stop looking at them for some reason, consider investing in a pair of blue-light-blocking glasses to wear before bedtime. I say ban TV from the bedroom because it's best if your brain associates your bed with sleep and not Netflix. If you need some sort of entertainment to help you relax, read a book instead.

When you're turning down the lights before bed, turn down the thermostat as well. The temperature of your bedroom can make a significant difference in your sleep quality. According to the Sleep Foundation, the best bedroom temperature for sleep is approximately 65 degrees Fahrenheit (18.3 degrees Celsius). This may vary by a few degrees from person to person, but most doctors recommend keeping the thermostat set between 60 and 67 degrees Fahrenheit (15.6 to 19.4 degrees Celsius) for the most comfortable sleep.

Caffeine and Alcohol

If you've been operating on both sleep debt and stress debt for years, you're probably also relying heavily on caffeine to get you through the day.

Don't panic, I'm not going to tell you to give up your beloved caffeine altogether, but you do want to stop caffeine consumption at least six hours before bed. It takes at least six hours for our body to process caffeine and get it out of our system, so that is important for good sleep hygiene.[17]

I'm often tempted to have a Diet Coke for dinner, but I've set a rule for myself that if it's after 3 p.m., I have decaf tea or water. My neuroscientist friend and mentor, Shonté Jovan Taylor, calls this a "caffeine curfew." Diet Coke in the evening isn't even an option in my mind anymore. Since there's no debate, it's easier to resist temptation.

You probably already knew that caffeine close to bedtime wasn't wise, but did you realize that alcohol can also disrupt your sleep?

Despite being a central nervous system depressant, alcohol can hurt your overall sleep quality by causing imbalances in your slow-wave sleep and REM sleep.[18] This imbalance decreases overall sleep quality, which can result in shorter sleep duration and more sleep disruptions. Alcohol might help you fall asleep faster, but to reduce the risk of sleep disruptions, you should stop drinking alcohol at least four hours before bedtime.[19]

I know this might be a hard one to believe—I struggled with this advice myself. Many of my friends enjoy a glass of wine in the evenings as a way to wind down, and it can certainly feel relaxing at the time. For me, it was margaritas. At one point, I was having one at home nearly every night, thanks to an amazing mix I had found. I enjoyed the taste, and as much as anything, it was a habit. It was part of my end-of-the-day routine, and I was admittedly hesitant to give it up even after reading the research.

But then I purchased an Oura ring, which is an advanced sleep tracker. I became somewhat obsessed with tracking my sleep and noticing trends. It very quickly became clear that on nights when I had a drink, my resting heart rate was higher and lowered later in the night. This directly impacted my sleep quality. After seeing the numbers and the clear correlation, I couldn't deny the science anymore, and since I valued a good night's sleep more than I valued the nightly margaritas, I gave them up.

That's not to say I never drink, but it's not a regular routine anymore. It's just not worth it to me to disrupt my sleep most days. When I do drink, I try to make sure it's at least four hours before bed if at all possible to minimize the effects.

If you don't own a sleep tracker, just try to pay attention to how rested you feel in the morning after drinking alcohol the night before versus when you didn't drink. It may surprise you to learn that even one drink can greatly impact the quality of your sleep as it did for me. Although everyone is different, in general, the closer to bedtime you drink and the more you consume, the more negatively it can impact your sleep quality.

To wrap this up, here's a little extra motivation to help you reconsider that nightcap. When your bloodstream has a mix of available energy sources, your body gives alcohol the VIP treatment. To put it simply, you have to burn off all the alcohol you've consumed before your body can start using energy from other sources, such as fat. In this regard, energy from alcohol is similar to sugar—your body gives it preference and metabolizes it quickly.[20]

So, not only is alcohol messing with your precious sleep, but it's also throwing a wrench into any weight loss plans you may have. *Talk about a double whammy!*

Exercise

In the next chapter, we'll delve into the many benefits of regular exercise. But before we dive into that, let's talk specifically about how exercise can positively impact your sleep. According to Charlene Gamaldo, MD, medical director of Johns Hopkins Sleep Disorders Center at Howard County General Hospital, studies show that exercise can help you fall asleep faster and improve the quality of your sleep.

Research suggests that as little as 30 minutes of moderate aerobic exercise can make a difference in sleep quality that very same night. Exercise can help you reduce stress and quiet your mind, leading to more restful sleep. Additionally, it can increase the amount of deep sleep you get, which is the stage of sleep where your brain and body have a chance to recharge.

Do be mindful of when you work out. Although there's no one-size-fits-all answer, most doctors recommend exercising no later than one to two hours before bed, if not earlier. Exercise can increase endorphins and body temperature, making it more difficult to fall asleep if you exercise too close to bedtime. And good news—morning workouts will still improve your sleep quality, despite occurring early in the day. So, if you're having trouble sleeping, consider incorporating some physical activity into your day to see if it makes a difference.

Reduce Stress

Do you ever get into bed, only to toss and turn, thinking about all the things you didn't get done today, what went wrong, and what you have to do tomorrow? If so, you're not alone.

There's even a phenomenon referred to as "evening anxiety" where some people get more stressed at the end of the day, as if all of their worries finally catch up with them. When my anxiety was at its worst, that was certainly true for me. I would make it through the day with varying degrees of success, crawl into bed exhausted, and promptly have a panic attack. It was awful. It felt like my body was punishing me for finally taking a break.

Researchers actually believe that at least 50 percent of insomnia cases are emotion or stress related.[21] That's why when we find outlets to reduce our stress, we often find that better sleep results.

So, how do you reduce stress and anxiety? Well, to start, focus on the four keystone habits covered in this book. Remember, I chose these four habits because they all reduce stress levels.

I will add a few more suggestions here, however, that helped me specifically with reducing anxiety and getting to sleep at night.

Put Pen to Paper

The first idea is to keep a notebook beside your bed. Every night, before you get into bed, take a moment to do a brain dump in the notebook and get anything and everything that's on your mind out and onto paper. It could be things on your to-do list tomorrow, something worrying you, or ideas you don't want to forget. Just get it all out so you don't lie in bed worrying that you will forget something on your list tomorrow. Once you have it all written down, tell yourself that you've done all you can for today and will handle the rest tomorrow.

If this sounds basic, know there's a lot of science to back it up. Research shows that writing out your to-do list for five minutes before bed can help you fall asleep significantly faster.[22]

Numerous studies have shown that journaling can reduce overall levels of depression.[23] A 2006 study by Stice, Burton, Bearman, and Rohde showed that writing in a journal can be as effective as cognitive behavioral therapy when it comes to reducing the risk of depression in young adults.[24]

Studies have also shown that journaling can reduce the frequency of intrusive, depressive thoughts, help college students who are vulnerable to depression, and reduce overall levels of depression in those diagnosed with a major depressive disorder.

There are also benefits of journaling for anxiety symptoms. One study by Hasanzadeh, Khoshknab, and Norozi found that the simple act of journaling reduced anxiety in women who were suffering from multiple sclerosis.[25] Another study found that journaling could help students effectively manage stress and anxiety, as well as improve overall classroom engagement.

Military Sleep Method

Another thing that has really helped me clear my mind to fall asleep is breathing deeply while progressively relaxing my entire body. It's called progressive relaxation because you start by relaxing your facial muscles and then relax your shoulders and keep working your way systematically down your body, relaxing one area at a time while breathing deeply.

This is also sometimes referred to as the "military sleep method" after going viral on TikTok as a technique that soldiers are taught to fall asleep fast anywhere. It appears to have first been shared in a book called *Relax and Win: Championship Performance in Whatever You Do*, by Bud Winter.

If I'm having too much trouble quieting my mind, it helps to use a guided meditation and focus on someone else's voice directing me. There are a ton of free phone apps you can use for this, including Calm and Insight Timer.

Tap It Out

The last tip I'll give here to help you relax if your anxiety is really bad before bed—or anytime, for that matter—is to use Emotional Freedom Techniques (EFT), also known as tapping.

EFT involves using your fingers to tap on nine points on your body (mostly on your head and face) while focusing on the issue troubling you. Addressing your anxiety on both the physical and mental levels simultaneously, EFT is highly effective.

Tapping is able to send signals directly to the stress centers of the mid-brain, according to researcher Dr. Dawson Church, which allows it to immediately lessen your anxiety.

With over 100 peer-reviewed studies on its effectiveness since its inception in 1995, EFT is a proven self-help technique. It has even been shown to be more effective than cognitive behavioral therapy, with fewer sessions needed for results in a large-scale study on anxiety and depression.[26]

There are countless tutorials on YouTube if you would like to learn EFT, or you can grab my free EFT guide at www.AFewGoodHabitsBook.com.

What If You Have a Bad Night's Sleep?

Okay, so now you know how to set yourself up for success, but what if you do everything "right" and still get a bad night's sleep? Because let's face it: We can't control everything, and not every night will be perfectly dreamy.

When bad nights happen, try these tricks to give yourself a boost:

1. Drink cold water with lemon first thing in the morning, before your coffee or caffeinated beverage of choice.

2. Get some sunshine. The light will kick-start the awake phase of your circadian rhythm and not only give you a boost in the morning but might help you sleep better that night.

3. Get some light exercise. If you're too tired for your normal workout, take it easier, but don't be a total couch potato. Remember, exercise will help you sleep better and reduce stress.

4. Take a power nap before 3 p.m. to reduce your sleep debt without messing up your sleep that night.

5. Prioritize. If you're truly exhausted from your bad night and not able to bring your A-game today, give yourself a break and let some of the little things on your list wait a day. Prioritize your most important tasks for the morning while you're still at your sharpest. And of course,

prioritize sticking to your bedtime routine tonight and try to turn in a little early if possible.

6. Summon your energy. We have more control over our energy than we give ourselves credit for. If you catastrophize and mope around saying how tired you are all day, well, you'll probably feel more tired! If you tell yourself that one bad night's not the end of the world and summon the energy to get through the day, you will probably make it through the day with more pep in your step.

Chapter 13

I LIKE TO MOVE IT, MOVE IT!

Exercise gives you endorphins. Endorphins
make you happy. Happy people just don't kill their
husbands. They just don't.
ELLE WOODS, LEGALLY BLONDE

We all know that exercise is essential for good health, but it's often the first thing to go when life gets busy. Work keeps many of us tied to our desks for long hours, with little time to move our bodies throughout the day. If you add nightly couch time to that, the time that your butt is firmly planted in a chair could easily reach 10 or more hours per day.

But here's the thing. We're not doing ourselves any favors by staying sedentary, and even small amounts of physical activity can have a significant impact on our health.

You may have heard some health experts call sitting the "new smoking" because a sedentary lifestyle can be as bad for your health as smoking. Research has linked prolonged sitting or other sedentary behavior to diabetes, poor heart health, weight gain, depression, dementia, and multiple kinds of cancer.[27]

In contrast, regular exercise has been shown to increase longevity, boost happiness as well as cognitive function, and improve health span—the number of years you can live without major diseases.

If you're worried that exercise and taking breaks will hinder your productivity, fear not! Research shows that exercise and regular movement can actually make you more productive.

Exercise has been shown to improve concentration, attention span, and alertness, which all contribute to better performance.[28] Plus, it improves learning, making it easier to retain information and apply it in your work.[29] So, although you might think you're losing time to exercise or taking breaks, the truth is that these activities can ultimately help you get more done.

Double Trouble

I want to pause and highlight the fact that there are two distinct issues when it comes to physical inactivity: lack of exercise and prolonged sitting. It's easy to lump the two problems together, but if you do, you risk neglecting a key aspect of your health.

Here's the deal. Some researchers have suggested that even if you're meeting exercise guidelines, sitting for long stretches can still mess with your metabolic health. That means we need to prioritize both exercise and movement throughout the day to stay healthy and sharp.[30]

Regular exercise and movement are not just good for reducing the risk of various diseases but also essential for improving mental focus, being able to learn more effectively, and reducing stress. So, if you truly care about your overall well-being and want to be your best self, you need to make exercise and movement a nonnegotiable part of your daily routine.

I get it—it can be tough to stay active with our busy schedules, and the thought of poor health outcomes may not be the most inspiring. The good news is that although some factors like genetics are beyond our control, we can modify other risk factors such as lifestyle choices to reduce our risk of chronic diseases.

Rather than dwell on what we can't control, we can focus on taking positive action to improve our health. Making exercise and an active lifestyle nonnegotiable is a great place to start. So, let's start prioritizing our health, one step at a time (literally)!

Daily Exercise Dose

Now, I'm not a health coach or a personal trainer, so I'm not going to tell you how to work out. What I am going to do is pass along some general recommendations from health professionals on how much exercise and movement we need to maintain a healthy lifestyle. Everyone's goals, health, and capabilities vary, and it's important to consult your doctor before changing your physical fitness routines.

As a general goal, the Mayo Clinic recommends that you aim for at least 30 minutes of moderate physical activity every day. If you want to lose weight, maintain weight loss, or meet specific fitness goals, you may need to exercise more.

For most healthy adults, the Department of Health and Human Services recommends the following exercise guidelines:[31]

- Get at least 150 minutes of moderate aerobic activity or 75 minutes of vigorous aerobic activity a week, or a combination of moderate and vigorous activity.

- Do strength training exercises for all major muscle groups at least two times a week. Aim to do a single set of each exercise using a weight or resistance level heavy enough to tire your muscles after about 12 to 15 repetitions.

One study found that following these guidelines reduces your risk of mortality by 21 percent.[32]

According to the Mayo Clinic, "Moderate aerobic exercise includes activities such as brisk walking, biking, swimming, and mowing the lawn. Vigorous aerobic exercise includes activities such as running, heavy yard work, and aerobic dancing. Strength training can include the use of weight machines, your own body weight, heavy bags, resistance tubing or resistance paddles in the water, or activities such as rock climbing."[33]

Bite-Sized Workouts, aka Exercise Snacks

Bite-sized, five-minute-or-less workouts have been dubbed "exercise snacks" and have become increasingly popular. Not only does research point to clear health benefits, but a short workout has obvious appeal to anyone who thinks they "don't have the time" to work out every day.

If you've not worked out in ages, 30 minutes of moderate physical activity every day might feel too intimidating to start with, or you might not see a way to fit it into your schedule right now.

If that's you, I've got some great news: It's okay to start small. You can start small by breaking the recommended 30 minutes into two or three short workouts instead of one longer workout and reap the same rewards. Still too much? Well, if you have even just two minutes per day, you can still see huge health benefits and decrease your risk of death by 18 percent.

This isn't just some crazy TikTok trend—there's research to back up the claims!

Doing a Little Can Help a Lot

Several studies have shown that even a small amount of physical activity can have significant benefits for overall health and longevity and may be even more beneficial than longer, less frequent workout sessions throughout the week.[34]

A study published in the *European Heart Journal* found that doing just 15 minutes of vigorous exercise per week, or two minutes of intense activity per day, can decrease the risk of death by 18 percent. The study monitored 71,893 adults for almost seven years and then kept track of who died over the course of the following five years. Those who did no physical activity had a 4 percent risk of death, and those who did just 10 minutes of exercise per week had a 2 percent risk over that time frame. Overall, 15 minutes of strenuous activity per week decreased the risk of death by 18 percent.[35]

A December 2022 study conducted by the University of Sydney found that even three to four one-minute bursts of intense activity per day can reduce the risk of premature death by up to 40 percent, and up to 49 percent for deaths related to cardio-vascular disease.[36]

These findings demonstrate that even a small amount of physical activity can have a significant impact on overall health and lon-gevity. If all we need is two to four minutes per day of exercise to reduce the risk of premature death, we truly have no excuses anymore! I'll be blunt: If you don't have time for a one-minute burst of activity four times per day, it's time to seriously reeval-uate both your schedule and your priorities.

How Intense Are We Talking?

I want to pause here and note that both of those studies on short workouts recommend vigorous or "intense" physical activity. You need to really get your heart pumping to get the full benefit of the exercise snacks—a stroll through your house won't cut it.

But how do you know what's considered intense? My definition of intense might be your walk in the park, after all.

There are three main ways to distinguish between moderate and vigorous activity levels, according to most sources: the rate of perceived exertion, the heart rate test, and the talk test.

The rate of perceived exertion is subjective and based on a scale from zero to 10, with moderate activity being rated 5 to 8 and vigorous activity being rated 7 or above.

The heart rate test measures how hard your heart is working and calculates a percentage of your maximum heart rate. Moderate exercise is 50–60 percent of your max heart rate, and vigorous exercise is 70–85 percent. To calculate your max heart rate, subtract your age from 220.

The talk test involves seeing if you can talk or sing while exercising. Moderate exercise should allow for talking but not singing, and vigorous exercise should make it difficult to say more than a few words.

Consistency is key when using any of these methods, so it's important to use the same tools or methods to measure progress over time.

I'll also restate the obvious: Remember to check with your doctor before jumping into any new fitness routine. They're the pros when it comes to keeping us healthy, while we're the pros at finding excuses to skip leg day!

Daily Movement

Now let's circle back to the importance of adding more movement in our days and reducing the amount of time we're sitting.

Don't forget that exercise is just one piece of the puzzle. It's not enough to simply clock in your 30-minute workout and then spend the rest of your day glued to a chair. Trust me, I'm not here to judge—I'm guilty of this too. As a fellow desk worker, I know the struggle is real. But the good news is that there are simple ways to reduce our sedentary time and make movement a part of our daily routine.

Now, you might be wondering, how often should we be standing up? Well, the research is mixed on this one. Some say every 20 minutes, and others recommend every hour. If that sounds like a lot, don't worry; even just a few minutes of standing and moving at regular intervals can make a big difference.

If you really can't leave your desk, at least stand up regularly and stretch for one to two minutes. If possible, take a walk down the hall or refill your water cup. You'll be surprised how much of a boost a quick break can give you, without taking up too much time or throwing off your workflow.

Based on the research I've read, I consider 60 minutes to be the maximum amount of time I should be sitting without a break. I have to admit that when I write that, it seems completely reasonable, but I know that in practice it can be challenging, especially if you have long meetings every day. So I am not suggesting that it's easy, but it's important nonetheless.

20-8-2 Rule

If getting up every hour sounds challenging, you're really not going to like what Alan Hedge, professor of ergonomics at Cornell University, has to say![37] Hedge recommends sitting 20 minutes out of every half hour at work, standing for eight minutes, and moving around for at least two minutes.

Following the 20-8-2 guideline means that you would be standing up and sitting down 32 times in a workday, which could have its own benefits.

Each time you do that, you are giving your body a "gravitational stimulus," reminding it of the effect of gravity, which can help muscles and bones stay strong, Hedge says. In the book *Sitting Kills, Moving Heals*, Joan Vernikos, former director of NASA's Life Sciences Division, talks about research suggesting that 32 transitions in a day help maintain healthy blood pressure.

In chapter 16, I reveal strategies to make your habits a reality and not just wishful thinking, but for now, here are a few suggestions specific to getting more movement into your day.

Timers to Remind You to Move

Staying active throughout the day can be a real challenge, especially when we're deep in concentration at work. But fear not, I have a super-simple solution: alarms!

Without a reminder, it's easy to get lost in our work and forget to move our bodies. I'm very guilty of this, believe me. But after reading up on the dangers of prolonged sitting, I knew I needed to make a change. So, I started using alarms to remind myself to get up and move every hour.

I first used the timer on my phone, but I found that I would sometimes forget to set it. That's when I bought a stand-alone timer. There are many options available online, from visual timers to classic kitchen timers, so you can find one that works for you.

To make it a habit, create an "if-then" rule for yourself. For example, "If I sit down to work on a project, then I set a 60-minute timer on my phone." When the timer goes off, I take a quick break to stand up, stretch, and move around.

To make sure I don't forget to use the timer, I place it between my keyboard and the edge of my desk before I stand up. That way, it's impossible to ignore when I sit back down.

So, if you're struggling to stay active during the day, give alarms a try. It's a simple and effective way to remind yourself to get up and move, even during your busiest workdays.

Make Small Changes

Daily movement doesn't have to be structured or complicated, either. The truth is, you can make a significant impact on your health by simply making small changes to your daily routine. Little changes add up!

For example, you could

- walk or ride your bike for short trips instead of driving.

- use the stairs instead of the elevator or escalator.

- get off the bus one stop earlier and walk the rest of the way.

- park farther away from your destination for a longer walk.

- make things you frequently use less convenient to reach so that you have to get up and move instead of just reaching across the desk to get them.

- purchase a standing desk and work standing at least two hours a day.

- if you really want to take it up a notch, purchase a tread-mill to go under your standing desk so you can walk while you work.

- take walking meetings instead of sitting while you talk. When meeting in person, you can walk around the building or the block with the person. If you're on a phone call or even Zoom, put in some earbuds and walk while you talk whenever possible.

- put on your favorite TV show and go for a walk on the treadmill for some Netflix and sweat time.

- make family outings active ones, like going for a hike together or playing tennis. Not outdoorsy or athletic? No problem! Going to a zoo, museum, or amusement park can add up to a lot of steps in a day!

Exercise Snack Ideas

Need some ideas for what those mini-workouts could look like? I've got your back! Here are a few ideas to try out. You can of course modify them to suit you and use them to inspire more ideas:

- Go up and down the stairs a few times.

- Take your dog for a jog around the block.

- Do squats for a minute while you're folding laundry.

- Do leg lifts while you're lying on the floor playing with your kid or pet.

- Do 20 calf raises while you're waiting in line or getting ready in front of the mirror each day.

- Stand up from your desk and run in place or do mountain climbers for a minute if you can't walk away.

- Do squats or jumping jacks while the water is warming up for your shower.

- Do push-ups while waiting for your coffee to brew in the morning. If you don't want to get on the floor, do them by leaning against the wall.

- Do a 5–10-minute high-intensity interval training routine in the morning. HIIT workouts can really pack a punch and wake up your brain and body at the start of the day without taking much time.

Remember, regular exercise is one of the most powerful keystone habits because of the huge ripple effect it can have on your life, even helping you get a better night's sleep. That's why, if I had to choose just one habit for you to start with, it would be exercise.

Chapter 14

WHERE FERRIS BUELLER GOT IT RIGHT

Make sure your worst enemy doesn't live
between your two ears.
LAIRD HAMILTON

I have to admit, I've had a bit of a love-hate relationship with meditation over the years and am far from an expert on the topic. I'm not a meditation teacher, a Zen master, or a yoga teacher. Because of that, I actually hesitated to include mindfulness and meditation as a habit in this book, to be completely honest. However, when it came time to choose the habits that I believe can have the biggest ripple effect on your life, I couldn't deny that mindfulness and meditation had to be included.

Since I'm not a master of meditation techniques, my goal here isn't to advocate for a particular style of meditation as much as it is to share the basic principles and benefits of mindfulness and meditation that I've learned over the years. Then, armed with this knowledge, you will be able to decide which style of meditation is right for you and explore further. I will, however, give you some basic practices to start with so that you can begin to develop foundational habits.

What's the Difference?

There is a ton of information about mindfulness and meditation on the internet, but the terms are often used interchangeably and with little explanation. This can be super confusing when you're getting started—I know it was for me! Although they are related, mindfulness and meditation are not the same, so let's start with some basic definitions so we're speaking the same language.

In a January 2012 interview in *Time* magazine, Jon Kabat-Zinn, a prominent writer and creator of the Mindfulness-Based Stress Reduction program, defines mindfulness as "the awareness that arises through paying attention on purpose in the present moment—non-judgmentally."[38]

Meanwhile, *Psychology Today* defines meditation as "a mental exercise that trains attention and awareness. Its purpose is often to curb reactivity to one's negative thoughts and feelings, which, though they may be disturbing and upsetting and hijack attention from moment to moment, are invariably fleeting."[39]

Notice that Kabat-Zinn's definition of mindfulness focuses on a way of being in the present moment without judgment, whereas the *Psychology Today* definition emphasizes the formal practice of meditation to enhance one's state of mind.

Although there are many definitions of each concept, these two highlight the difference between mindfulness as a way of living and meditation as a practice. Mindfulness can be cultivated through many practices, including mindfulness meditation, whereas there are numerous categories of meditation beyond just mindfulness meditation.

Each type of meditation has distinct characteristics and techniques that guide the meditator toward diverse paths of personal development. Selecting a meditation practice involves understanding your objectives and what each form of meditation can offer.

Regardless of the style you settle on, there seem to be clear benefits. Studies have suggested that meditation and mindfulness can help people manage anxiety, stress, and depression, reduce pain, lower blood pressure, and improve both concentration and willpower.[40]

So however we define them, there's no doubt that both mindfulness and meditation are powerful habits that can help improve both physical and mental health, and lead to greater overall well-being and happiness.

Basic Definitions

Mindfulness is the practice of paying attention to the present moment, without judging it or getting distracted by thoughts or emotions. It involves being fully present and aware of what is happening both inside and outside of ourselves and can be practiced in many different ways, such as through meditation, breathing exercises, or simply focusing on the present moment during daily activities.

Meditation is a set of techniques that are designed to promote mindfulness and relaxation through targeted focus. This focus can be directed toward different elements such as repeating a specific mantra, monitoring the rhythm of our breath, or even concentrating on the flame of a candle. Examples include mindfulness meditation, which encourages attention to the present moment, and mantra meditation, which involves recitation of a word or phrase to aid concentration. Regular practice of meditation can help us cultivate a calmer, more focused mind, better equipping us to stay present and engaged in our daily lives.

What's the Point of Meditation?

As I mentioned, I've had a love-hate relationship with meditation over the years. When I first heard meditation described, I was incorrectly told that it was about "clearing your head of all thoughts." Not only is that basically the *opposite* of the real goal of meditation, but it's also an impossible challenge. You will literally never be able to completely stop your mind from having thoughts. It's like trying to will your heart to stop beating—it's not going to happen and it's not a smart goal to focus on.

Since I thought the goal was to clear my mind of all thoughts, I thought I was terrible at it, would get super frustrated, and would end a meditation session more anxious than I had started it. *No wonder I hated it!*

Nevertheless, because I kept hearing about all the benefits of meditation, I kept trying for a while, thinking I'd get better with practice. Finally, I gave up, feeling like a failure because I could never "clear my mind" and reach the blissed-out, relaxed state I was after.

Years later, someone much wiser explained that having a completely blank mind was not the goal. The goal is to notice the thoughts that come up (because they will) and then let them float on by and return to focusing on your breath or mantra, depending on your meditation style.

Let me say that again—the practice is to notice the thoughts but then mindfully return your focus to where you want it to be rather than getting hooked on the thought or feeling that came up and heading down the rabbit hole.

That's literally the point—to practice returning your focus again and again and again—as many times as you have to—to where you want it to be (for example, your mantra) instead of being totally at the mercy of your distracted, emotional brain.

So if the practice is returning to the mantra and you have a super-busy mind that keeps getting distracted, that's awesome, because you're going to get a ton of practice at noticing and returning to your mantra. If you spend an entire 10-minute meditation session doing nothing but catching yourself having random thoughts and then returning to the mantra, then you, my friend, have just had a really awesome meditation practice! You got a lot of reps in, and that's a win!

Why It's a Keystone Habit

To keep things simple, I'm bundling together mindfulness and meditation as one keystone habit. As you can see, they are technically two separate things, but because of the way they're interconnected, I believe we can link them together, much like I bundled together exercise and movement. (Meditation purists will just have to forgive me on this one.)

The reason I believe meditation and mindfulness are powerful enough to be considered one of the handful of core habits you should focus on is the ripple effect they have on your mental and physical health. In particular, they have the ability to reduce stress, help you better focus your mind, and strengthen your willpower muscle.

Way back in section 1, we talked about how you can't rely solely on willpower to meet your goals. That's why I'm going to give you a ton of techniques to lean on in chapter 16.

However, anything we can do to strengthen our willpower is a win and will improve our chances of making good decisions and sticking to our habits. So how do mindfulness and meditation practices help increase willpower? you ask. Great question!

Remember I told you that the point of a meditation practice is to return to your mantra or breath again and again, as many times as you need to? That's essentially willpower practice!

You're tempted by a distracting thought, you notice it, and you choose to focus on what you really want to instead. You're training your brain to notice temptation, remind yourself of your goal, and then choose a preferred action instead.

You're getting a lot of "self-control reps" in every time you meditate, a practice that's transferable to the rest of your life. The next time you start to mindlessly reach for a cookie when you're trying to lose weight, you can tell yourself, *Ahh, this is like when I'm meditating. This is good practice!* Don't beat yourself up. Just notice what happened with something akin to scientific curiosity and detachment, and then make the choice to return your focus to where you want it to be—on your goal of losing weight and making healthy food choices.

That is mindfulness. Remember, Kabat-Zinn defines mindfulness as "the awareness that arises through paying attention on purpose in the present moment—non-judgmentally."

When I Started Really Seeing the Benefits of Meditation

When I started to see meditation as willpower practice and as a way to be more mindful in everyday moments, I really started to see the value in it.

Until that point, I honestly struggled to see clear benefits in my day-to-day life. Once I learned I didn't have to clear my mind, I would meditate and feel more relaxed afterward, but I wasn't sure it necessarily carried over into the rest of my day. At one point, I committed to an eight-week meditation practice. I remember telling a friend I wasn't really sure if it was helping. I expected it to work like some sort of magic pill that could make me calmer and less reactive throughout the day after just 10 minutes of practice in the morning. Maybe it did, maybe it didn't, but let's just say I wasn't dazzled by my results.

When I stopped looking to meditation only as a way to relax, I not only enjoyed it more but was able to draw a really clear line between the mindfulness practice I was getting during a session and how I could use it during the rest of my day.

I wanted to highlight this particular benefit to mindfulness meditation because even though there's a ton of research and a lot of talk about the benefits to your mental health and stress reduction, it was only recently that I saw a direct line between these practices and self-control.

Long story short, starting a mindfulness and meditation practice and making it a habit has countless benefits for your mental and physical health. If you're like me and haven't been impressed by the calming effects of meditation in the past, give it another try, and this time, keep the benefits to your willpower top of mind. You might become a convert like me.

Meditation Basics

I can't speak to all the meditation styles out there (remember, not a meditation teacher!), but the way I've been taught is to focus on either your breath or a mantra. Your mind needs something to focus on and return to when you get distracted. So before you begin, decide if you will keep your mind focused on your breathing or it would be more helpful to focus on a mantra.

As a beginner, I felt like having a mantra was super helpful, and I usually still use one. I had one meditation teacher recommend using a Sanskrit word as a mantra because you don't even need to know or fixate on its meaning to use it. For example, I used the word *swaha*, which the teacher said means "surrender."

Brendon Burchard has a practice he refers to as the Release Meditation Technique that I enjoy. The basic idea is to close your eyes, repeat the word *release* to yourself over and over again, and, as you breathe deeply, release any tension you're holding on to. You do that by letting go of any thoughts causing tension but also by using the progressive relaxation technique I described in the chapter on sleep habits. Burchard recommends using this technique to transition between activities throughout your day.[41]

For example, if you answer emails for 30 minutes and are ready to move on to creating a presentation, rather than diving right in, take two minutes to close your eyes and do the Release Meditation. Before you open your eyes, set an intention for how you want to feel as you work on your next task. (What energy do you want to bring to the work? How do you want people to feel when they hear it?)

For a more detailed explanation of the Release Meditation Technique, you can find Burchard's video explainer at www.AFewGoodHabitsBook.com.

Step-by-Step

Now for some basics on how I meditate. I'm honestly not sure if there's a name for this style; it's just a mash-up of all I've learned about how to meditate over the years and what I've found to work well for me. If you're a complete beginner to meditation, I hope it will help. If you're already an advanced meditator, well, don't laugh at this very basic description of how to meditate!

Find a comfortable spot to sit with your back supported and your head free. In the beginning, I think it's helpful if you can have some peace and quiet. I don't recommend trying to meditate in the middle of the morning craziness as your whole family is running around getting ready. That being said, you don't need absolute quiet either. Any noises can serve as another chance to return your focus to the mantra instead of as frustrations that make you give up.

I like to start with a mindfulness practice to help me settle in. I close my eyes and take 10 deep breaths, focusing on an extended exhale, which helps calm the nervous system. (Inhale for a count of four, hold for seven, exhale for eight.)

Then I tap into each of my five senses one at a time.

- **What can I see**—even with my eyes closed? *(Some light coming in from the window through my closed eyelids.)*

- **What can I hear?** *(A dog barking in the distance. A ticking clock.)*

- **What can I feel?** *(My soft sweater. The cushion under me. The warmth of the sun coming through the window. The tension in my shoulders.)*

- **What can I taste?** *(My toothpaste.)*

- **What can I smell?** *(My coffee. The flowers on the counter.)*

Then I try to hold all five senses together at once for a few moments—sight, sound, touch, taste, and smell. Because I've brought everything so much into my awareness, it's easier for me to accept anything I notice during meditation. They feel less like distractions and more like senses I invited in.

Next, I bring my attention to my mantra—or you can focus on your breathing. I repeat the mantra gently in my mind, over and over again. I have to repeat it quite frequently to start or my mind immediately gets distracted before I can even begin.

Don't think of the mantra as a way to "beat back" thoughts, though; think of it more like a tool to guide you toward what you want. I sometimes imagine I'm walking down a path toward deeper relaxation with the mantra floating on the wind ahead of me, coaxing me forward.

Inevitably, a stray thought will pop up. Remember, that's totally normal and just how our brains work. Not only that but *yay!* You have a chance to get some willpower practice in now!

Don't judge the thoughts that come up—or yourself for having them. When you catch yourself thinking about errands you need to run or the mistake you made earlier, just think, *Ahh, interesting, there's a thought,* and then let it float on by, almost like a passing cloud floating through your mind. Then just return to your mantra as many times as you need to.

I like to wrap up the practice with gratitude and intention setting. *(What am I grateful for, and what are my intentions for the day? What energy do I want to bring to my activities and interactions today?)*

You don't have to practice for hours on end. Start with five minutes or even just two minutes. Once it has become a habit, you can slowly increase the time if you want, but you don't have to meditate for hours for it to be helpful. Personally, I never meditate for more than 15 minutes at a time. Just find a length that feels good to you. Something is better than nothing!

Types of Mindfulness Practices

As you've seen, one of the ways I use mindfulness is to get myself calm and focused on the present moment before I begin to meditate.

I also use the five senses mindfulness practice separate from meditation anytime I find my thoughts are starting to spiral with what-if scenarios and worries about the future. It's the exact same process, though I do keep my eyes open when I am tapping into my sense of sight.

When I am anxious, being able to focus on things in my environment feels very grounding. I usually look for five green things in the room to give myself something specific to focus on other than what's worrying me. I start slowing down my breathing while I do this and then, if possible, shut my eyes as I tap into the remaining four senses both to help my concentration and to give my brain a visual break.

There are plenty of other ways to practice mindfulness as well, such as eating mindfully, walking mindfully, or even having mindful conversations. Active mindfulness practices involve participating in everyday activities with the goal of being mindful. That includes taking things slow, being attentive, holding off on judgments, and completely immersing yourself in your current experience.

Take a Turtle for a Walk

Love the idea of having a mindfulness practice but can't seem to remember to do it? I hear you, I struggled with that too—until I learned a funny little historical fact. Apparently, at one point in the 1800s in Paris, it was fashionable to take a turtle to the park for a walk. It was an attempt to slow down and appreciate the moment—in other words, it was a mindfulness practice.

Something about the mental image of taking a turtle for a walk—perhaps on a leash, me taking baby steps through the park behind the turtle—is hysterical to me.

How does this help? I started adding "walk the turtle" to my to-do list. It's a great visual that never fails to make me smile.

It's more fun than seeing "be mindful" on my list, and therefore I am more likely to actually do it. (No turtle required.)

Guru Bueller

The next time you go for a walk, whether it's to walk your dog, go hiking, or just walk from your car to the store, take a moment to slow down a bit and really pay attention to your surroundings. You'll probably be surprised by what you notice. We're always so busy rushing from one activity to another that it's easy to overlook the small beauties in our days.

As Ferris Bueller wisely said, "Life moves pretty fast. You don't stop and look around once in a while, you could miss it."

PLANNING ISN'T JUST FOR PARTIES

Nothing is less productive than to make more efficient
what should not be done at all.
PETER DRUCKER

In chapter 7, when you did a reality check on your life, you might have realized that your actions aren't always congruent with your intentions—that there are areas where you say you want something, but you don't fully commit and take action. You made a choice, but you haven't really decided to make it happen.

We've already discussed some possible reasons for this, such as relying on willpower and motivation. There's another very basic reason this happens, and that's a lack of planning. And more specifically, not planning with intention.

When I speak about intention here, I really want to focus on two things:

1. being intentional and specific when creating your plan

2. being mindful of how you want to show up and behave while pursuing your goals

Simply put, intentions are not only about the plan and the steps you take to achieve your goals, but also about how you show up and behave along the way. Your attitude and behavior are factors that can mean the difference between success and failure.

Relationship Intentions

Let's start by talking about setting intentions for how you want to show up for the people in your life. Think about your most important relationships. How do you want to behave with the people who matter most to you? How do you hope people feel in your presence?

Think this through one person at a time, because every relationship is different.

For example, if you were very intentional about being fully present with your kids so that they knew they were a top priority for you, what would that look like exactly?

- How would you speak to them? What would your tone be?

- How would you describe the energy you bring to family time? What would you like it to be?

- When you see them, what words would you focus on to remind you of your intention and how you want to show up for them?

- How do you want them to feel while you're together and afterward?

If you're just going through the motions, showing up and trying to survive each day—that has a certain energy to it. That energy will affect how you behave and speak to people.

Let me be clear, though—this isn't about trying to be perfect and get it right every time. It's about having really clear intentions about how we want to show up in each situation and then reminding ourselves again and again and again, every single day, of those intentions.

The clearer we are and the more we remind ourselves of how we want to behave, the more likely we are to act congruently the majority of the time. When we keep our intentions at the forefront, we're less at the mercy of our ever-changing emotions and more in control of our actions.

Think of the last time you argued with someone you care about.

- What was your intention for the conversation?

- Did you even have a clear outcome you hoped for?

- Did you just barrel into the conversation focused on what you wanted and why, or did you take time to think things through first?

- Did you consider how you could get them on board with your idea and how it could be a win-win?

In my experience, the more intentional we are about how we speak to the people in our lives and the more intentional we are about the energy we bring to our relationships, the happier we tend to be. It might seem like an obvious statement, but in reality, we don't always take the time to be intentional in our closest relationships.

You can use if-then statements to help you be more intentional with your relationships.

"If I see my partner, then I will think _______." "If I see my daughter, then I will remind myself _______." "If my mom calls, then I will focus on _______."

The easiest ball to drop when it comes to relationships is, unfortunately, with the people who love us most. I've definitely been guilty of this. When I was struggling in 2020, I knew I couldn't lose my cool at work, but on some level, I knew my husband and kids would give me grace if I wasn't showing up as my best self at home. No one ever intends to yell or lose their patience with the people they love—I certainly didn't—but that's the point. I didn't focus enough on showing up intentionally with my family and wasn't always able to keep my cool as a result.

I was really struggling with anxiety and depression and completely overwhelmed. I could make excuses, and I've made my apologies, but I still have regrets about how I showed up during that time. All I can do now is be more intentional about how I show up moving forward.

There's a lot I wish I could change about 2020, but one of the lasting lessons was definitely about being more intentional in my most important relationships—especially when times are hard.

Scenario-Specific Intentions

Setting intentions is not just limited to your relationships. It can also be a powerful tool to help you navigate common scenarios in your life and important events. For example, before heading into a meeting or any important event, it can be helpful to take a moment to ask yourself how you want to show up and be with people. What kind of energy do you want to bring into the room? By setting an intention, you give yourself a sense of direction and purpose, whether it's to remain calm and patient or to be strong and decisive.

I've learned through my own experience and coaching that when you enter every situation with an intention, you're more likely to be happy with the outcome, even if things don't go exactly as planned. Setting intentions helps you take control of your thoughts and actions, and this sense of control can lead to better outcomes in various areas of your life. Of course, setting intentions doesn't guarantee that everything will go your way, but it does improve the odds that you'll walk away feeling satisfied with how you showed up.

Planning with Intention

When working toward our goals, it's important to take a step back and reflect on how we want to approach the activities and tasks that will help us get there. Ask yourself, *How do I want to show up as I complete these tasks?* Consider how you want to feel and the thoughts you want to focus on while you're getting your work done.

It's also important to make sure you're prioritizing the right things. Are you spending your time and energy on the activities that will truly make a difference and move you closer to your goals—or are your days filled with busywork?

This includes carving out time on your calendar for important but not necessarily urgent tasks, such as long-term planning or skill-building activities. By being intentional and strategic about how you approach your goals and the activities required to achieve them, you can increase your chances of success and minimize wasted time and energy. Taking the time to set yourself up for success in this way can help you stay focused, motivated, and on track toward achieving your desired outcomes.

Tips for Planning

Okay, now for the nitty-gritty details of actually getting your priorities on the calendar! I recommend planning the coming week on either Friday afternoons or Sundays.

Personally, I do my planning on Sundays after I've had some time to rest and process anything that went on during the previous week. It takes only about 10 minutes, so it doesn't really take away from my free time, and it allows me to get mentally prepared for the new week. If for any reason you tend to dread Mondays, taking this time to plan and set intentions on Sunday can help you eliminate the so-called Sunday Scaries that some people feel as well.

I know other people who love to do this planning on Friday afternoons. The logic here is that Friday afternoons tend to be slow, and planning can be a good change of pace and a way to put a bow on the week. Plus, it doesn't interrupt your free time and you can head into the weekend feeling confident you have everything under control—or at least a plan of action for the following week.

Whatever you do, don't wait until Monday morning to plan the week! I tried it one week and felt behind from the get-go. My day didn't go nearly as smoothly. Not to mention, you run the risk of missing early-morning meetings or other priorities for Monday.

Block Out Time

When you're planning, don't just look at the meetings and commitments to others on your calendar. Be sure to block out uninterrupted time to move forward with your most important priorities. This includes your work priorities but also any healthy habits like exercise and other personal priorities you've set.

Review Your Schedule and Set Reminders

Review your schedule every morning, and set reminders and alarms. When I am working and get into a flow state, the time flies, and I not only forget to stand up and move but run the risk of missing meetings. To make sure that doesn't happen, I rely on timers and alarms. I set an alarm for five to 10 minutes before every meeting so I have time to prepare. I also set a 60-minute timer every time I sit down so I remember to get up and move throughout the day.

In addition to my meeting and movement alarms, I have reminders of my intentions that pop up throughout the day. You can do this by labeling alarms or setting reminders on your phone. There are also phone apps you can use to pop up reminders at set times or intervals.

I have a repeating reminder that simply consists of the three words I've chosen to focus on, that I hope describe the best of who I am and how I want to show up. My words are *patient, kind,* and *joyful.* What are your three words? How can you remind yourself regularly how you want to show up in the world?

Another tip is to label your meeting alarms with your intention words. On the iPhone, at least, you're able to name the alarm. So instead of just setting an alarm for my 2 p.m. coaching session, I might label it with *enthusiasm*, *recognition*, and *outcome focused*, for example.

Using Implementation Intentions

Habits can be triggered by any number of cues such as hearing a phone notification ding, seeing yummy doughnuts in the break room, or noticing your running shoes laid out in the morning. However, the two most common triggers are time and location.

By using implementation intentions, you can leverage these two triggers to help establish a habit. Essentially, implementation intentions involve making a plan for when and where to act to successfully implement a particular habit.

This should sound familiar. Remember the study I mentioned in chapter 10 and how the successful would-be exercisers used implementation intentions? All they did was fill in the blanks on the following sentence: "During the next week, I will partake in at least 20 minutes of vigorous exercise on [day] at [time] in [place]."

Just having this basic plan of action made the difference between success and failure. It's the difference between hoping to work out and making it a habit.

The simple way to apply this strategy to your habits is to fill out this sentence:

I will [behavior] at [time] in [location].

- I will meditate for two minutes at 8:30 a.m. at my desk.

- I will plan my week at 3 p.m. on Sunday in the kitchen.

- I will read for 20 minutes at 9 p.m. in bed.

- I will take a 10-minute walk at 2 p.m. around the block outside my office building.

If you want your habits to stick, give them a time and a space to live in. By doing this consistently, your brain will start to recognize the pattern and you'll begin to feel a natural urge to do the right thing at the right time, even if you don't know exactly why. It's all about creating those strong associations!

Broadly speaking, the format for creating an implementation intention is "When situation X arises, I will perform response Y."[42]

So, for example, you could also state an intention as "When I transition between work tasks, I will do the Release Meditation Technique before starting the new task."

Another example might be "When I get up, if the weather is too bad to run outside, then I will get on the treadmill instead."

Don't just think of these implementation intentions—write them down. They should be added to your calendar when you plan the week.

If there's one thing I've learned this year, it's that you can never have too much detail on your calendar. If something isn't on my calendar, it's not likely to happen. It's just a dream, not a goal, and it has no hope of becoming a habit.

If you have a habit you want to make a priority, put it on the calendar. Especially when starting a habit, don't assume you'll remember without a reminder.

Preparing for Challenges and Dodging Decision Fatigue

Before we jump into the next chapter full of practical ideas to help your habits stick, let's have a friendly chat about two key things: getting ready for challenges and dealing with decision fatigue.

First up, don't forget the importance of planning for those occasional setbacks. If you think you need a refresher, feel free to check out chapter 9 again. The main idea is to know what to do when things don't go as planned. Work out in advance how you'll handle failure and temptations, and how you'll decide when to either throw in the towel or keep moving forward. By creating if-then plans for your most important habits, you'll make those tough decisions a whole lot easier.

Now let's talk about decision fatigue. Various internet sources estimate that adults make an average of 35,000 decisions each day.[43] I'm not sure how accurate that number is, but researchers at Cornell University have found that we make 226.7 decisions each day about food alone, so it's probably not too far off![44]

With that many daily decisions happening, it's no surprise we can feel overwhelmed at times. To stay focused on what really matters, it's wise to reduce the number of smaller, everyday choices you have to make. You can do this by planning, setting up if-then scenarios, and crafting intentions that make your top decisions the simplest and most obvious options. By doing this, you'll set yourself up for habit success while keeping your mental energy intact.

Chapter 16

WHERE THE RUBBER MEETS THE ROAD

Good habits are worth being fanatical about.
JOHN IRVING

Sprinkled throughout the book, I've given you ideas for how to make your desired habits happen. Now I want to bring it all together so that you can clearly see the "rules" for habit creation, the strategies you can leverage, and which ones should be your go-tos for each of the four good habits we've discussed.

The Rules of Habit Creation

There are five key concepts or rules you always want to keep top of mind while you're establishing new habits:

1. Make It Easy.

2. Start Small.

3. Make It Specific.

4. Make It Fun.

5. Make It a Vote for Your Desired Identity.

Make It Easy and Start Small

When establishing a new habit, you want to make getting started as simple as possible. You can do this by making the action easy to do and as small as you can. Think baby steps to ease you into the new habit.

Let's use starting a new exercise routine as an example. How can you make that easier to do every day?

- Set out your workout clothes the night before.

- Put your running shoes by the door.

- Work out at home so you don't have to go anywhere.

- Go to the gym on your way home from work so you don't have to go out again after you get home.

- Choose a gym that's directly on your usual route so you don't have to go out of your way to get there.

- Follow along with an exercise video so you don't have to figure out what to do.

Continuing with the exercise routine, how could you start small?

- Start with "exercise snacks" instead of full workouts.

- Start with just one exercise snack per day and then slowly increase the number per day.

- Instead of starting with walking for an hour, start with walking to the end of the block and back.

- Need to start even smaller? Make your first goal just to put on your exercise clothes every day. That's it. That's the goal. If you work out, awesome, but the first goal is just to change into workout clothes, period. Establish that habit first and then work your way up to actually exercising.

Basically, how can you make your goal so ridiculously small that it would be silly *not* to make time for it? Start there and make that a habit first. As long as you take the tiny action, you've met your goal. The reality is, once you get started, you will likely want to go further. That's great, go for it if you want to, but the goal is just to establish the habit of taking the first tiny action. Make that a habit and you're more likely to keep up the routine. Some experts recommend forcing yourself to do *only* the tiny habit at first and not allowing yourself to go further until you feel like you've really nailed the tiny step.

Make It Specific

We've talked a lot about making your goals specific. Let's pull it all together now with three ways to make your goals more clearly defined.

1. Implementation Intentions

2. Failure Planning

3. Setting a Floor and a Ceiling

Implementation Intentions

As a reminder, implementation intentions involve making a plan for when and where to act to successfully implement a particular habit.[45]

To use this strategy for your habits, just complete either of these sentences:

"I will [behavior] at [time] in [location]."

"When situation X arises, I will perform response Y."

The more detail you can have in your implementation intentions, the better, so that there's no vagueness. You want to be 100 percent clear on what you will do when and for how long or how much.

Here are a few sleep routine examples:

"I will avoid using my phone in bed and read a book instead at 9 p.m. in my bedroom."

"When I feel restless at night, I will practice deep breathing and progressive muscle relaxation to calm my mind and body."

Failure Planning

We've talked a lot about why planning for obstacles, temptation, and failure is important, but let's nail failure planning down even more with an actual process. (This process is adapted from Benjamin Hardy's book *Willpower Doesn't Work*.)[46]

1. Write down your top goal.

2. Give it a deadline, preferably one not too far in the future.

3. Imagine all the potential obstacles you'll face in achieving that goal and write them down.

4. Now write down if-then responses for each of those obstacles.

5. Write down the conditions under which you will absolutely quit.

Make your if-then responses as specific as possible. One of the advantages of carefully planning out what failure might look like and what you will do is that you're more likely to take action to prevent failure long before things get too bad.

Under what conditions will you quit? Will it be based on how you feel, on the amount of time invested, or on results? Only you can make that call—there's no one right answer here.

Examples of if-then responses:

- If I find myself getting distracted during meditation, then I'll gently bring my attention back to my breath without judgment or criticism.

- If I sleep poorly and don't have the energy for the cardio workout I had planned, then I will do yoga instead.

- If my partner and I have a disagreement, then I'll take a few deep breaths and remind myself to listen actively, stay calm, and express my thoughts and feelings with empathy and respect.

- If I find myself getting distracted by my phone, then I'll put it in the other room until my work is finished.

Floors and Ceilings

Setting minimums and maximum limits for your behaviors is another way to get specific with habits. Author Steven Huskey talks about setting limits in the form of "floors" and "ceilings."

A floor is the minimum amount of a specific action you will do, and a ceiling is a maximum. Floors help establish tiny habits, and ceilings can help break unhealthy ones. By setting limits, you can better control your time, money, energy, and effort.

The floor is a lower limit—you'll do no less than this. Here are some examples:

- Do at least one push-up per day.

- Work out at least three days per week.

- Meditate for no less than five minutes per day.

- Spend at least 30 minutes outside per day.

- Get no less than seven hours of sleep.

- Spend at least five minutes stretching every morning.

The ceiling is an upper limit—you'll do no more than this. Here are some examples:

- Spend 30 minutes or less on Facebook each day.

- Check email no more than twice per day.

- Watch TV for no more than one hour per day.

- Eat red meat no more than twice per week.

- Sit for no longer than 60 minutes without getting up to move.

Make It Fun

Starting new habits and chasing after our goals should be fun and enjoyable! I'll admit that I've forgotten this before when

I'm trying to reach my own goals, but it just ends up making me feel burned out. Take it from me: If you can make the process more enjoyable, you're more likely to stick with your habits and have a good time doing it.

Everyone's idea of fun is different, but let me share two stories that might give you some inspiration here.

I worked with a coaching client who shared that between her attention-deficit disorder (ADD) and her rebellious nature, she both hated routines and knew she'd benefit from them. Lana's ADD made it hard for her to remember to get things done, but she hated the idea of having the same routines day in and day out. Part of the reason she became an entrepreneur was to have more freedom in how she spent her time. She couldn't deny that her lack of routines and healthy habits were starting to hurt her personally and professionally, though.

In addition to sharing practical planning tips, I helped Lana change how she thought about routines and brainstorm ideas to make them more fun and enjoyable. Lana loves all things magical and mystical, so instead of thinking of her healthy morning routines as obligations or tasks to check off a list, she began to think of them as rituals she could infuse with some magic. And just like magic, she was suddenly much more consistent with her habits!

I used the same tactic when I worked with another client, Terri, who suffered from anxiety. She had so much fear and anxiety around driving and running errands, it was starting to limit her independence and even impact her relationship because she was becoming so reliant on her partner. Terri loves sci-fi and fantasy books and movies, so she began to see running errands as epic quests she was embarking on. *It's not just a trip to the pharmacy, it's an adventure!* Sure, there might be challenges along the way, but that's what makes the hero's journey interesting, right? Using her imagination to make these outings more interesting helped take her mind off of the anxiety-inducing aspects and gave her the courage to get out of her comfort zone.

Whether you have ADD, anxiety, or just need the motivation boost, making your habits fun will always make it more desirable to maintain them.

Think about the habits you want to establish. How can you make them more fun—either in how you think about them or how you actually perform them?

Take exercise, for example. If you hate running or going to the gym, what could you do instead to meet your exercise goals that would be more fun?

- You could learn how to Hula-Hoop.

- You could have dance parties every evening with your kids.

- You could have push-up contests with your partner.

- You could learn a new sport and get competitive about it.

- You could walk on a nature trail instead of on a treadmill.

- You could watch your favorite TV show while on the treadmill and make that the only time you're allowed to watch it.

The possibilities are endless! Think about the habits you want to start. How can you make them more fun or enjoyable?

Make It a Vote for Your Desired Identity

Your habits are how you embody your identity. In fact, the word *identity* is derived from the Latin words *essentitas*, which means "being," and *identidem*, which means "repeatedly." So your identity is literally your "repeated beingness."

In chapter 10, I spoke briefly about tying your goals and habits to your identity. James Clear, author of *Atomic Habits*, advocates for creating "identity-based habits" by focusing on who we wish to become, not what we want to achieve.

Remember, Clear says, "It's one thing to say I'm the type of person who *wants* this. It's something very different to say I'm the type of person who *is* this."[47]

So, when I think about my goals, I ask myself, *What type of person could get the outcome I want? What type of person could lose 30 pounds?* Well, it's probably someone who is consistent, for one thing. They'd be consistent with their exercise routines and consistently stick to their food plan.

These questions help reveal the identity I want to work toward and the habits that support that identity. It shifts the goal from losing 30 pounds (outcome based) to being the type of person who's consistent with their exercise and eating habits (identity based).

If every action is a "vote" for the type of person we'd like to be, as Clear says, then the most practical way to change who you are is to change what you do.[48] New identities require evidence. Every time you take an action, it provides you with proof that you are that type of person.

As a day-to-day practice, this could be as simple as asking yourself *What would a healthy person do?* every time you have a choice to make. Would a healthy person order a salad or a bacon cheeseburger? Would a healthy person take the elevator or the stairs?

The good news? Just like a candidate for office doesn't need to receive 100 percent of the votes to win an election, you don't have to be perfect with your actions to ultimately "win" and meet your goals. You just have to keep casting votes for the person you want to be the majority of the time to get the outcomes you want.

How to Leverage Environmental Design

In chapter 2, we discussed the impact our environment has on shaping our actions and outcomes. New information, new experiences, and new relationships help us grow, evolve, and adapt. Our environments shape us, so it's our job to cultivate the ideal environments for both challenge and recovery. When we leverage our environment, we don't have to rely solely on our willpower or motivation to meet our goals and stick to our habits.

In addition to surrounding ourselves with the people and experiences that can help us grow, we can leverage our environments by using cues and reminders, as well as forcing functions.

Forcing Functions

Forcing functions are a simple but powerful way to help you achieve your goals by making it easier to take action. They work by removing the option to make certain mistakes *(Whoops, I'm on Facebook again!)*, freeing up your brainpower to focus on what matters most.

Instead of relying on willpower or constantly reminding yourself to stay on track, you create an environment that naturally supports the habits you want to create.

Forcing functions help to build an environment that naturally supports the behaviors you want. They work in a way that, with just one major decision, can make your future choices easier or even unnecessary. Having endless options isn't always a good thing. How can you simplify things, remove options that aren't really serving you, and make the "easy" option the one that will support your good habits?

Forcing functions can be game changers when it comes to productivity, because they help you stay on task without having to constantly battle your own impulses.

Forcing functions come in many shapes and sizes. From the fear of consequences to hefty up-front investments, from the pressure of social accountability to the thrill of a new challenge, forcing functions can give us that extra push we need to reach our goals.

A simple example of how to use forcing functions is to delete phone apps you compulsively use or to put your phone out of reach while you're working. And let's not forget the power of a good old-fashioned deadline—nothing like a ticking clock to light a fire under us! So, whether you're facing a tough project or trying to form a new habit, consider using a forcing function to help you rise to the challenge and bring your A-game.

A Change of Scenery

Another simple way to tap into the power of your environment is to seek out a change of scenery. According to research by Dr. Ellen Langer, the very act of changing environments can dramatically increase your energy levels. More energy can improve focus, creativity, and productivity.

You can change things up by working in different spots in your home or office throughout the day or by getting out of your usual work environment altogether and working in another location for a while. Try working from a coffee shop, library, or park to change your scenery and get a new perspective.

Alternatively, if you don't want to leave your workspace (or aren't able to), you can try rearranging or redecorating your space. Move your desk to another wall and bring in some plants or art—anything to make the space feel different.

When we work in the same space day in and day out, it's easy to show up and mindlessly go about our routines. By changing the environment we work in, we make it far easier to bring more mindfulness and presence to our days. And of course, this idea doesn't have to be limited to your workspace.

Take a moment to think of other areas of your home or office where you might want to make some changes. Where would it serve you to shake things up a bit? How might a change to the environment either help you disrupt a bad habit or start a new one?

A few ideas to get you thinking:

- Store tempting sweets out of sight, or keep them out of the house entirely.

- Make your bedroom a more peaceful, relaxing space to make falling asleep easier.

- Clear out clutter from your workspace or living area to create a more organized and calming space.

- Change the lighting in your workspace or living area to create a different mood or ambience.

- Create a designated meditation or yoga space in your home to encourage daily mindfulness practices.

- Try standing or walking meetings instead of always sitting at a desk.

- Create a cozy reading nook in your home to encourage more reading and relaxation.

- Use noise-canceling headphones or a white noise machine to block out distractions and create a more focused environment.

Triggers, Reminders, and Cues, Oh My!

A costly mistake many of us make is relying on our working memory (aka short-term memory) to remember all the things we need to do. Costly because not only are we likely to forget something, but we're also wasting valuable brain space on remembering a lot of random information that could instead be used for creative pursuits and problem solving. Fortunately, there are some easy solutions to this problem—intentional planning, and the use of triggers and reminders.

Triggers or cues, whichever you prefer to call them, are situational and environmental reminders that help make your habits easier to remember and more automatic. I like to use situational triggers to remind me of the if-then scenarios I've created.

For example, if I'm waiting in line, I do a quick check of my energy levels and attitude. If I am not happy with what I find, what can I do to improve them? Waiting in line serves as the trigger to do that check.

Another type of mindfulness cue is a doorway trigger. You can create a general if-then scenario for all doorways, or create prompts for specific situations. Here are some examples:

If I walk through my front door, then I remind myself that I want to be patient and attentive with my family.

If I walk through the conference room door, then I bring a positive attitude and an open mind so that I can be a true leader to my team.

If I walk through any doorway, then I center myself and summon my best.

I learned about triggers in Brendon Burchard's book *High Performance Habits.*[49]

You can use other physical reminders to help you stay on track with your habits, such as sticky notes, alarms, and notifications, or even something you wear, like a necklace, that reminds you of your goals and how you want to show up. I have a bracelet that says "Find the Joy" on it to help me remember to always look for the upside and to raise my energy levels and bring joy to every situation.

What I have found with physical reminders like these is that I have to mix them up occasionally, because after a while I become "blind" to them. If the habit has become completely ingrained and automatic by that point, that's fine. If it hasn't, move around your physical reminders or change them in some way so they get your attention again.

Anchoring, aka Habit Stacking

Anchoring is a special type of implementation intention that involves linking a new habit to an existing one instead of to a specific time and place. Developed by BJ Fogg as part of his Tiny Habits program, this approach can create an effective trigger for almost any habit. If you follow the work of James Clear, you likely know this method as habit stacking, but whatever you call it, it works![50]

The reason habit stacking works is that it builds on your existing habits. Think of the things you do every day without even thinking about them. Things you would never forget to do, like brushing your teeth, showering, or putting your makeup on. What new habit could you "stack" on top of the existing habit?

James Clear recommends using this formula:

After/Before [current habit], I will [new habit].

- After I finish work for the day, I will take a 20-minute walk outside.

- After I wake up, I will stretch for five minutes.

- Before I turn on my computer in the morning, I will look over my schedule and set my intentions for the day.

- After I finish my morning shower, I will visualize my goals for the day.

- After I pour my cup of coffee each morning, I will meditate for two minutes.

- Before I get into bed at night, I will set out my exercise clothes for tomorrow.

- After I finish a task, I will take a two-minute break to breathe deeply and release tension.

Ways to Use Intentional Planning

We discussed intentional planning in the last chapter, so let me give you a quick recap of how to use it, and then I will give you a few new planning tips as well.

Ways to be more intentional while planning:

- Set relationship intentions for the most important people in your life.

- Set scenario-based intentions for important events, meetings, and touchpoints in your day.

- Be intentional and strategic about the goals you set and how you're showing up while you work toward them.

- Schedule time for the important, needle-moving activities on your list, not just the urgent tasks.

- Plan the week ahead on Friday or Sunday afternoons.

- Block out uninterrupted time to move forward with your most important priorities.

- At the start of your day, set your intentions for how you want to show up and the attitude and energy you want to bring.

- Think through any challenges you foresee in your day and how you want to handle them. Set your intentions and also have your "failure plan" decided on so you know how you want to proceed.

- Set alarms and reminders for your meetings, blocked-out project time, and movement breaks each day.

- Master your transitions between tasks by taking a quick break to get up and move, release tension, and set your intentions for the next task.

- Make sure your implementation intentions are on your calendar. If your goals don't have a time and place on your calendar, they are less likely to happen.

One more planning note as well as a new idea for you . . .

When it comes to planning out your days, I don't believe it's possible to include too much detail. What I have found is that the more detail I can put into my daily schedule, the better.

For example, my goal is to check email only three times per day, so I put "check email" on my to-do list three times and check them off as I go. In addition to making sure the task gets done, having it on my list serves as a reminder of the ceiling I've put on this activity.

I've also found it very helpful to not just put "workout" on my calendar but to decide in advance what type of workout I will do each day. Since one of my goals is to vary my workouts, making the decision in advance means there's no debate about what to do that day and I am far less likely to fall into a rut and not challenge myself.

Last but not least, consider time tracking, even if just temporarily. As an entrepreneur, I haven't had to track my time or report it to anyone for the past decade. That is, until I was going through my coaching certification program in 2020. One of the courses included a challenge to track your time all day, every day, for a week.

I admit that at first, I was annoyed by the idea. It felt like a huge hassle. But what I discovered while tracking my time was very interesting. There are a lot of fancy time-tracking apps out there, but I kept it simple and used a Google spreadsheet. Every time I started a new activity, I'd put it in a row on the sheet, noting the start time and then the finish time. I also categorized everything into some broad areas such as exercise and self-care, family time, client work, coaching time, and so on. The idea was to see how I was spending my time and if I had any semblance of balance.

The added bonus to the tracking, which I didn't expect, was that I quickly realized I was far less tempted to let distractions take me off course when I was tracking my time. I had a terrible habit of hopping from one task to another. I would hop from email to Facebook to Slack all within minutes. It was a multitasking nightmare! At the end of the day, I would feel like I'd worked like a madwoman all day but hadn't really accomplished much. I was getting things done, but I felt too scattered, so it didn't feel productive.

When I started time tracking, if a notification popped up while I was in the middle of something, I'd think, *Nope, I'll deal with that later. I don't want to have to start a new line on my time sheet.*

Tracking my time ended up being a huge blessing. Not only did I have much more awareness of how I was actually spending my time, but I became far more efficient with my work and got more of the important tasks done when I stopped multitasking. I already knew that multitasking was not an efficient way to work, but the time sheet was the tool that finally got me to commit to focusing.

All of that to say, consider manually tracking your time, even if for just one week, and see if it changes how you focus. If nothing else, you will gain a lot of insight into where your time is going each day. If it feels like a pain in the butt—good! That's not a bad thing in this case, because you will be far less likely to task switch.

Make It Happen!

There you have it! These are all of the many ways that you can make your goals happen. Creating good habits can be challenging, but it is possible with the right mindset and strategies. By implementing these ideas and tactics, you can create the positive habits that will help you achieve your goals and live the life you desire.

THE EXCITING CONCLUSION

We are what we repeatedly do. Excellence then, is not an act, but a habit.

WILL DURANT

When we started this journey together, I told you that the key to unlocking better days, less stress, and more success was to unlearn the BS stories you've been told about personal growth, uncomplicate things, and get back to basics.

Along the way, we unlearned a few things about the traps of overachieving, hustle culture, the need to know it all, and being endlessly self-sacrificing. We learned that willpower and motivation don't work. We learned that stress isn't even the enemy we've been told it is! *Who knew, right?* That's a lot of mind trash to unpack. It should be feeling a little lighter up in the ol' gray matter!

Next, we took an honest look at our lives to see where we might be a little out of whack and what needs some TLC. Taking the time to refocus and get real about where you are, what you want, and where you're headed is powerful—but it can also be confronting, so I want to recognize you for doing that work.

Not many people take the time to do this type of reality check, but I think the world would be a better place if we all did.

And then, of course, came the habits—regular exercise and movement, a solid sleep routine, intentional planning of your day, and meditation and mindfulness.

Five core truths emerged from all my research:

1. Real transformation takes place at the identity level.

2. Success lies in starting small and keeping things simple.

3. Planning is essential for success, and plans must be specific and account for potential failures.

4. Motivation and willpower are not reliable—you have to create an environment that sets you up for success.

5. It takes only a few good habits to change your life—the trick is selecting the right habits to focus on.

I think Jim Rohn said it best: "Success is a few good habits repeated every day. Failure is a few bad decisions repeated every day."

When I first decided to write a book that would combine all that I've learned about habits, stress, high performance, and personal development, I wasn't entirely clear how I was going to pull everything together, to be honest.

What I did know was that I wanted to create a practical guide for strivers like me. People who want to fulfill their potential and achieve big things—but without burnout and collateral damage to their personal lives. I feel like I've finally cracked the code on what that looks like—but it took me literally years to piece all the information together. It took me reading countless books, spending over $20,000 on coaching certification programs, and even more courses on top of that on topics ranging from nervous system regulation techniques to meditation to neuroscience and high-performance habits. It was like a very long, expensive scavenger hunt for knowledge.

I don't believe it should take anyone that much time or money to figure out how to prevent burnout and build the life they crave. I also knew that I had never seen anyone draw a clear link between stress relief, habits, and high performance—not all in one place and not as a practical guide. That's why it took me so long to put all the pieces together for myself, and that's what I hope I've done for you in this book—laid out a plan that is both practical and powerful in its simplicity.

At first glance, sleep and exercise routines, intentionally planning your days, and the use of mindfulness and meditation might seem "too basic" to focus on. I get it—trust me, there were certainly times when I thought, *Can I really write a whole-ass book about these basic practices?* At the end of the day, though, I kept coming back to two truths . . .

There's an amazing amount of power in uncomplicating things and getting back to basics. We don't need

razzle-dazzle—we need a plan that works and that we can actually accomplish.

And, of course, my favorite saying: Common sense isn't always common practice. Although the four habits might seem like basic commonsense advice, they're not always common practice. If you know these things in theory but you're not actually doing them, they can't help you.

With that in mind, I knew that my main objective was to make it abundantly clear *why* these habits matter and why you hear them come up again and again. Until the reasoning goes from a nebulous idea to something that actually matters to you, you won't take it to heart and make it a habit.

Not only that, but just wanting to do these things is not enough—otherwise we'd all be getting eight hours of sleep and be super fit, insanely productive, and as mindful as a monk every day. But we're not, because we need more than motivation and willpower to maintain even these so-called "basic" habits.

The last section of the book has given you all the tools you need to actually make these habits happen. The key is to *actually use them*. Don't be like I was and learn all of this stuff and not do anything with it for years.

The four good habits I've outlined truly are keystone habits that will have a positive ripple effect in your life and help reduce stress at the same time. The tools I shared really will make habit-change doable—but it's up to you to take the advice and run with it now.

Remember, the goal isn't a perfect, stress-free life. The goal is to live a meaningful life and leverage these tools to handle the stress that will inevitably come up along the way.

Don't try to do everything at once. Just take the habits one at a time and watch the dominos fall, one good thing leading to another. Start with exercise, then sleep. Exercise has been proven time and time again to have a hugely positive ripple effect. And if you're not getting at least seven hours—ideally eight hours—of sleep per night, you will be amazed at the difference that makes. As author JoJo Jensen said, "Without enough sleep, we all become tall two-year-olds," and we all know how unreasonable two-year-olds can be!

Spare Change Adds Up

When I was a kid, my parents had this enormous change jar. It must have been two feet tall, and was made of dark, thick glass. I have no idea where they got it, but at the end of every day, my dad would come home with change in his pockets and dump it into the jar. Anytime there was spare change in the house, it went into the jar.

Mind you, this was back in the '80s and '90s when people still paid for things mostly in cash, so we had change to toss in pretty regularly. A quarter here, a few nickels and pennies there. Nothing big. Not enough to seem significant, for sure, yet every year we'd sit down and roll change, and lo and behold, we'd have a couple of hundred dollars. All that spare change added up to something pretty significant.

I'd sort of forgotten about the enormous change jar from my childhood, but then I was reading Jon Acuff's book *Soundtracks*, where he equates the idea of saving up spare change to taking baby steps toward your goals. Every little bit counts. Something about the analogy really stuck with me.

It's easy to poo-poo the idea of taking tiny steps forward and working on what feels like really basic habits. It can feel insignificant, like, "Will it *really* make a difference if I just take a 10-minute walk? Will it *really* make a difference if I just work on this project for 20 minutes instead of two hours?"

I can definitely be an all-or-nothing kind of girl, so I get it. If I'm not going to put on the fancy workout clothes and hit the gym for an hour, is it even worth it? If I can write only 500 words today instead of 2,000, should I even bother?

The short answer is *yes*. Take the baby step. Save the 40 cents. Write the paragraph. Walk around the block twice during lunch. Reach out to one person who might be able to help with that project instead of trying to work up the energy to call 10 today. Meditate for five minutes instead of an hour.

Take the step. Baby steps are a big freakin' deal when you're stuck in analysis paralysis. When you're in a shame spiral and completely overwhelmed, a baby step can feel like Mount Everest, I get it. I'm here to say that if you're in that place and you take one tiny step today, not only will it add up, but I'm cheering for you like a crazed mom at a T-ball game, jumping up and down with a tear in my eye like, "Hells yeah! You've got this!"

As you begin to implement the advice in this book, remember—spare change adds up. It all counts. Done is better than perfect and you have to start somewhere, so don't discount small steps.

And if it helps, have a secret little laugh and picture me jumping up and down, cheering for you while you're working on your habits. I'd be honored to be your very own, slightly less nerdy, definitely more sweary version of Stuart Smalley in your head.

Hells yeah! You've got this!

YOUR MISSION, SHOULD YOU CHOOSE TO ACCEPT IT . . .

Beyond these last pages, your thoughts have the potential to shape the future of this book and hold the power to ignite endless possibilities for another reader.

You've journeyed through *A Few Good Habits* and emerged richer in knowledge, and are well on your way to becoming a habit hero. I hope you had a few laughs, learned a lot, and are ready to get to work on your habits!

Now, can I interest you in one more adventure? Your next mission, should you choose to accept it, involves navigating the wilds of the Amazon—the .com, not the jungle.

Your quest? Leave a review!

Just like a trusty map aids an explorer, your review serves as a guide for this book in the literary wilderness. By leaving a review, you're not only sharing your valuable insights but also helping *A Few Good Habits* find more readers like you.

A review is the perfect offering for the algorithm gods, elevating this book's visibility, which is invaluable for independent authors like me.

Plus, who doesn't enjoy wielding such power from the comfort of their own couch? Go ahead, drop a review, and add "literary superhero" to your list of accomplishments. You'll certainly be my hero!

Thank you for your incredible support!

Scan to leave a review on Amazon

SUMMARY GUIDE AND DEFINITIONS

Habit is the intersection of
knowledge (what to do), skill (how to do),
and desire (want to do).

STEPHEN R. COVEY

This summary guide is intended to help remind you, at a glance, of all that you've learned and the tactics you can leverage for each of our four good habits and their definitions.

A Few Good Habits to Change Your Life

The four keystone habits that can have far-reaching ripple effects on your mental, emotional, and physical health, as well as your productivity and success:

1. Sleep routines

2. Regular exercise and movement

3. Intentionally planning your days

4. Mindfulness and meditation

Anchoring (aka Habit Stacking)

Anchoring is a special implementation intention involving linking a new habit to an existing one instead of to a specific time and place, using this formula to create an anchor: **After/Before [current habit], I will [new habit].** Example: After I wake up, I will stretch for five minutes.

Change of Scenery

You can change things up by working in different spots in your home or office throughout the day, by redecorating or rearranging your space, or by getting out of your usual work environment altogether and working in another location for a while. A change to the environment can also help you disrupt a bad habit or start a new one.

Environmental Design

Environmental design is the art and science of creating an environment that sets us up for success by removing the need for excessive willpower. It goes beyond just the physical space we inhabit and includes the people we surround ourselves with, the information we consume, and the food we fuel our bodies with. When we create an environment that encourages growth and evolution, we're more likely to achieve our goals and be our best selves.

We can do this by creating environments that are optimized for both productivity and rest. On one hand, we need spaces that motivate and inspire us to produce our best work. On the other hand, we also need to create environments that allow us to recharge our batteries and recover from stress and exhaustion.

Forcing functions leverage environmental design and are a powerful tool that allows us to simplify decision making and avoid making certain mistakes. By making one decision that makes all other decisions easier or irrelevant, we can eliminate decision fatigue and make it easier to achieve our goals.

It's all about setting ourselves up for success by shaping our environment to support our goals and dreams.

(See also Change of Scenery and Forcing Functions.)

Exercise Snacks

Exercise snacks are bite-sized, five-minute-or-less workouts that can pack a big punch in terms of health benefits. Several studies have shown that even a small amount of physical activity can have significant benefits for overall health and longevity and may be even more beneficial than longer, less frequent workout sessions throughout the week. This is your permission slip to start small and a reminder that something is better than nothing when it comes to getting your daily movement in.

Failure Planning

Benjamin Hardy's process[51] for failure planning:

1. Think about your top goal.

2. Write down your top goal.

3. Give it a deadline, preferably one not too far in the future.

4. Imagine all the potential obstacles you'll face in achieving that goal.

5. Write those obstacles down.

6. Now come up with an if-then response for each of those obstacles.

7. Write down your if-then responses to all the obstacles you imagined.

8. Write the conditions in which you will absolutely quit.

Floors and Ceilings

A floor is the minimum amount of a specific action you will do, and a ceiling is a maximum. Floors help establish tiny habits, whereas ceilings can help break unhealthy ones. By setting limits, you can better control your time, money, energy, and effort. The floor is a lower limit—you'll do no less than this. For example, do at least one push-up a day. Work out at least three days a week. The ceiling is an upper limit—you'll do no more than this. For example, spend 30 minutes or less on Facebook each day. Check email no more than twice a day.

Forcing Functions

Forcing functions are simple but powerful tactics that make it easier to take action by removing the option to make certain mistakes (like mindlessly scrolling through social media when you should be working). By freeing up your brainpower to focus on what really matters, you can make progress toward your goals with less effort.

There are numerous types of forcing functions you can use, such as consequences for poor performance, high up-front investments, social pressure, difficulty, novelty, and real deadlines. By making one key decision that simplifies all other decisions, forcing functions eliminate decision fatigue and help us stay on track toward our goals.

If-Then Statements

If-then planning is a type of implementation intention. It is a strategy that involves deciding in advance what action to take in response to a specific situation. Creating if-then statements helps you mentally prepare yourself to handle whatever life throws at you so that you can stay on track. By anticipating potential roadblocks and developing a clear plan to overcome them, you'll be less likely to give in to temptation or make impulsive decisions. This can help you reduce decision fatigue, increase self-control, and automate healthy behaviors, ultimately making it easier to achieve your goals.

Examples of If-Then Statements:

- If I feel thirsty, then I will drink water instead of sugary drinks or soda.

- If I have a craving for something sweet, then I will have one piece of dark chocolate instead of a candy bar.

- If I feel bored, then I will go for a walk outside or do some other physical activity instead of snacking.

Identity-Based Habits

Identity-based habits focus on who we wish to become, not on what we want to achieve. When you think about your goals, ask yourself questions like *What type of person could get the outcome I want? What type of person could do X?*

Implementation Intentions

Implementation intentions involve making a plan for when and where to act to successfully implement a particular habit.[52]

To use this strategy for your habits, just complete either of these sentences:

"I will [behavior] at [time] in [location]."

"When situation X arises, I will perform response Y."

The more detail in your implementation intentions, the better, so that there's no vagueness. You want to be 100 percent clear on what you will do when and for how long or how much.

Intentional Planning

- Set relationship intentions for the most important people in your life.

- Set scenario-based intentions for important events, meetings, and touchpoints in your day.

- Be intentional and strategic about the goals you set and how you're showing up while you work toward them.

- Schedule time for the important, needle-moving activities on your list, not just the urgent tasks.

- Plan the week ahead on Friday or Sunday afternoons.

- Block out uninterrupted time to move forward with your most important priorities.

- At the start of your day, set your intentions for how you want to show up and the attitude and energy you want to bring.

- Think through any challenges you foresee in your day and how you want to handle them. Set your intentions and also have your failure plan decided on so you know how you want to proceed.

- Set alarms and reminders for your meetings, blocked-out project time, and movement breaks each day.

- Master your transitions between tasks by taking a quick break to get up and move, release tension, and set your intentions for the next task.

- Make sure your implementation intentions are on your calendar. If your goals don't have a time and place on your calendar, you're less likely to make them happen.

- Track your time to see how you use it and as a way to keep you focused on the task at hand.

- Include a lot of detail on your calendar about what you are doing each day. Get super specific about what you will do and when. Include your ceiling and floor limits.

Intention Setting

When I speak about intention setting, I focus on two things—being very intentional with your daily planning and being very intentional about how you want to be as you go about your day.

In other words, intentions are about not only your plan and the steps that will take you there, but how you intend to show up—your way of being and behaving as you go after your goals. Set relationship intentions to help guide your interactions with the important people in your life. Set scenario-specific intentions for important meetings and situations that arise. For example, before heading into a meeting or any important event, it can be helpful to take a moment to ask yourself how you want to show up and be with people. What kind of energy do you want to bring into the room? By setting an intention, you give yourself a sense of direction and purpose, whether it's to remain calm and patient or to be strong and decisive.

Reminders

Physical reminders can help you stay on track with your habits. Sticky notes, alarms, and notifications are easy ways to set reminders. You could also get creative and use something you wear, such as a necklace, that reminds you of your goals and how you want to show up.

Rules of Habit Creation

There are five key concepts or rules you always want to keep top of mind while you're establishing new habits: Make It Easy, Start Small, Make It Specific, Make It Fun, and Make It a Vote for Your Desired Identity.

Triggers and Cues

Triggers, aka cues, are situational and environmental reminders that help make your habits easier to remember and more automatic. I like to use situational triggers to remind me of the if-then scenarios I've created. You can create triggers for the important people and situations in your life. Doorway triggers and waiting triggers can help remind you to be intentional about how you're showing up with the people and events that are important to you.

ABOUT THE AUTHOR

Julie Lowe is an author, speaker, and Certified High Performance Coach on a mission to help you take your life from ordinary to outstanding—without sacrificing your sanity. Julie's wisdom is grounded in neuroscience, but it's her unique mix of warmth, empathy, and wit that makes her coaching sessions feel like a breath of fresh air, leaving her clients not just enlightened but motivated and empowered.

Self-proclaimed taco connoisseur and Marvel fanatic, Julie is living her best life in Lexington, Kentucky, with her husband, two sons, and a trio of rescue dogs.

Julie's expertise has earned her recognition in top media like Yahoo! Life, the *Huffington Post, Good Morning Washington, The List, GOSS* magazine, and *Authority Magazine,* to name a few.

She's also an avid blogger, and has been sharing her insights into everything from personal growth to habits, productivity, marketing, and entrepreneurship since 2013.

Follow Julie on social media and check out her blog for inspiration and practical tips—and when you're ready to take a quantum leap with your lifestyle, explore Julie's coaching services to experience the power of high-performance coaching firsthand.

Website: www.CoachJulieLowe.com

Facebook.com/CoachJulieLowe

Instagram.com/CoachJulieLowe

Book Website and Resources: www.AFewGoodHabitsBook.com

ACKNOWLEDGMENTS

I am overwhelmed with gratitude for all the people who supported me throughout the writing of this book! As a lifelong lover of books, I can tell you that becoming a published author is truly a dream come true—but I couldn't have done it without support.

First and foremost, I want to thank my amazing husband, Eric Lowe, for his unwavering support and encouragement. You are my rock, and I couldn't have chased my entrepreneurial and author dreams without your love and support all these years.

To my sons, Jacob and Josh, thank you for inspiring me to be my best self and for loving me unconditionally as I've worked to balance growing my business and our family over the years. I don't always get it right, but you always give me grace. I want you both to know that no dream is too big and no challenge is too great when you put your hearts and minds into it. Remember that true success is about more than just achieving your goals—it's about finding joy and fulfillment in the journey and making a positive impact on those around you. I am forever grateful for your love and proud to be your mother. Thank you both for reminding me what's truly important in life.

I want to thank my mom, Jill, for instilling in me a love of books and reading that has been a constant source of inspiration throughout my life. Thanks to my dad, Steve, for teaching me the value of hard work and perseverance and to my brother, Jim, for keeping me humble and reminding me to laugh and not be too serious. Thank you to my in-laws, Mary and Donnie, for your love and support and for welcoming me into your amazing family all those years ago.

To my pre-readers, Shay Jordan Hrobsky, Cassie Shea, Kim Schroeder, Lanette Pottle, my husband, Eric, and everyone on the launch team: Your feedback and support were invaluable, and I'm so grateful for all that you did to help bring this book to life.

A huge thank-you as well to my friend and graphic designer Brad Wilson for designing the logo for Dog-Eared Prose & Press. I also want to thank Ashley Hinson Dhakal for the book cover design and page layout work.

A special shout-out to my book coach, Lanette Pottle of She Gets Published, who guided me through the writing and publishing process with expertise and enthusiasm. Your belief in me gave me the confidence to realize my dream, and I can't thank you enough. And of course, a huge thank-you to my editor,

Laurel Robinson, whose sharp eye and editorial wizardry made this book even better than I ever thought possible.

Thank you as well to all of my friends, family, clients, and followers who have been cheering me on and believing in all of my crazy dreams for the past decade of my entrepreneurial journey. No matter what I pursue, I always know I have a faithful set of supporters at my back, and that is priceless. The fact that there are too many of you to name is a true blessing. I do want to recognize in particular Shay Jordan Hrobsky and Shannon Myers, my dear friends whom I can't imagine doing life without. Thank you as well to Kim Caloca-Madden, who has been a part of my team since the beginning and who helps keep the wheels spinning behind the scenes at Socially Aligned.

To my furry companions—Pippa, Sally, and Zoey—who never judge me for stress-eating at my desk during deadlines (as long as you get a bite). Thanks for always being by my side, even when it means sitting through endless hours of me typing away at my computer.

To all my current and past clients worldwide, I want to express my heartfelt gratitude for your trust in working with me. It has been an honor and a privilege to serve each of you and help you achieve your goals. I am grateful for the opportunity to learn from you, to grow with you, and to make a positive impact on your lives. Thank you for the invaluable lessons and experiences, and for being a part of the journey that led to the creation of this book. I'm looking forward to many more years of guiding and supporting incredible people like you on their journey toward success.

Finally, I want to acknowledge the writers and researchers whose work paved the way for mine, particularly Brendon Burchard, James Clear, Kelly McGonigal, Charles Duhigg, and Benjamin Hardy. Your insights and ideas greatly informed this book, and I'm grateful for your contributions to the field. Thank you as well to all the coaches and mentors who have helped shape my business over the years, including Marisa Murgatroyd, Jen Gottlieb, Chris Winfield, Juliana Frisoli, Lexi D'Angelo, Brendon Burchard, and Nisha Moodley. Special thanks to neuroscientist and coach Shonté Jovan Taylor, founder of the OptiMind Institute, who added her insights to the sleep habits chapter. I'm lucky to call you both a friend and a mentor, and I am so happy I took my work to the next level by studying with you to become a NeuroCoach!

And to all of you, dear readers: I am truly grateful for your unwavering support and enthusiasm as I brought this book to life. Thank you for purchasing the book, sharing it with friends, and writing reviews that help others discover it. Your encouragement and kindness have meant the world to me and have made this journey so much fun.

As you close this book and embark on new adventures, I would love to stay in touch with you. Follow me on social media and subscribe to my newsletter to stay updated on new projects and opportunities. Thank you once again for being a part of this incredible journey.

WORK WITH JULIE

Are you ready to supercharge your success in both your personal and professional life? Julie Lowe is here to help you do just that. You've already discovered the power of science-backed practices in *A Few Good Habits*, so just imagine the transformation you could experience with personalized one-on-one coaching!

Julie teaches ambitious professionals how to prioritize their mindset, health, and relationships—without sacrificing the quality of their work.

We all want to prioritize our families and health, but we also don't want our work to suffer. So, we try productivity hacks that "free up" our time . . . which we proceed to fill with more work. We essentially just get more efficient at burning ourselves out!

Or we plan vacations that provide only temporary stress relief and connection with loved ones. But let's be honest: We're going to work overtime before and after the vacation to "make up for it" . . . so is the time away really that helpful and relaxing?

Clearly, this isn't sustainable: It ends in either burnout or the destruction of our personal lives. If you're crushing it at work but dropping the ball at home, you're not actually a high performer. You're just a high achiever at work. But there's good news: Your work doesn't need to result in collateral damage to a healthy personal life—or vice versa.

What if we could apply the same high-achieving attitudes, habits, and principles that make us so successful at work to our personal lives? Then we would live in a way that's congruent with our values—more energized at work, and fully present at home.

In her programs, Julie will teach you or your team how to become true peak performers: successful and fulfilled at both work and home, without sacrificing either for the other.

Ready to get started? Visit CoachJulieLowe.com to learn more.

Interested in bulk ordering A Few Good Habits or booking Julie for speaking engagements or workshops? Email julie@coachjulielowe.com.

REFERENCES

1   Brendon Burchard, *High Performance Habits* (Carlsbad, CA: Hay House, 2017), 14–15.

2   Ellen Langer, *Mindfulness* (Boston: Da Capo, 2014), preface to the 25th edition.

3   Kelly McGonigal, "How to Make Stress Your Friend," filmed March 2013 in Edinburgh, Scotland (TEDGlobal, 2013), 14.16, https://www.ted.com/talks/kelly_mcgonigal_how_to_make_stress_your_friend/.

4   Abiola Keller, Kristin Litzelman, Lauren E. Wisk, Torsheika Maddox, Erika Rose Cheng, Paul D. Creswell, and Whitney P. Witt, "Does the Perception That Stress Affects Health Matter? The Association with Health and Mortality," *Health Psychology* 31, no. 5 (April 2011): 677–684.

5   Jeremy P. Jamieson, Matthew K. Nock, and Wendy Berry Mendes, "Mind Over Matter: Reappraising Arousal Improves Cardiovascular and Cognitive Responses to Stress," *Journal of Experimental Psychology* 141, no. 3 (August 2012):

417–422.

6   Kelly McGonigal, *The Upside of Stress* (New York: Avery, 2015), 86.

7   Sarah Milne, Sheina Orbell, and Paschal Sheeran, "Combining Motivational and Volitional Interventions to Promote Exercise Participation: Protection Motivation Theory and Implementation Intentions," *British Journal of Health Psychology* 7 (May 2002): 163–184.

8   Milne, Orbell, and Sheeran, "Combining Motivational and Volitional Interventions."

9   James Clear, *Atomic Habits* (New York: Penguin Random House, 2018), 74.

10   Peter M. Gollwitzer and Paschal Sheeran, "Implementation Intentions and Goal Achievement: A Meta-analysis of Effects and Processes," *Advances in Experimental Social Psychology* 38 (2006): 69–119, https://doi.org/10.1016/S0065-2601(06)38002-1.

11   Clear, *Atomic Habits*, 33.

12   Charles Duhigg, *The Power of Habit* (New York: Random House, 2012), 109.

13   Duhigg, *Power of Habit*, 109.

14   Institute of Medicine, ed. Harvey R. Colten and Bruce M. Altevogt, *Sleep Disorders and Sleep Deprivation: An Unmet Public Health Problem* (Washington, DC: National Acade-

mies Press, 2006), https://doi.org/10.17226/11617.

15   A. M. Williamson and Anne-Marie Feyer, "Moderate Sleep Deprivation Produces Impairments in Cognitive and Motor Performance Equivalent to Legally Prescribed Levels of Alcohol Intoxication," *Occupational & Environmental Medicine* 57, no. 10 (2000): 649–655, https://doi.org/10.1136/oem.57.10.649.

16   Christine Blume, Corrado Garbazza, and Manuel Spitschan, "Effects of Light on Human Circadian Rhythms, Sleep and Mood, *Somnologie 23, no. 3 (August 2019): 147–156, httsp://*doi:10.1007/s11818-019-00215-x.

17   Christopher Drake, Timothy Roehrs, John Shambroom, and Thomas Roth, "Caffeine Effects on Sleep Taken 0, 3, or 6 Hours Before Going to Bed," *Journal of Clinical Sleep Medicine* 9, no. 11 (November 2015): 1195–1200, https://doi.org/10.5664/jcsm.3170.

18   Timothy Roehrs and Thomas Roth, *Sleep, Sleepiness, and Alcohol Use. National Institute on Alcohol Abuse and Alcoholism* (Bethesda, MD: National Institute on Alcohol Abuse and Alcoholism, n.d.), https://pubs.niaaa.nih.gov/publications/arh25-2/101-109.htm.

19   Michael D. Stein and Peter D. Friedmann, "Disturbed Sleep and Its Relationship to Alcohol Use," *Substance Abuse* 26, no. 1 (March 2005): 1–13, https://doi.org/10.1300/j465v26n01_01.

20   Arthur I. Cederbaum, "Alcohol Metabolism," *Clinical Liver Disease* 16, no. 4 (November 2012): 667–885, https://doi.

org/10.1016/j.cld.2012.08.002.

21   Maurice M. Ohayon and Thomas Roth, "What Are the Contributing Factors for Insomnia in the General Population?" *Journal of Psychosomatic Research* 51, no. 6 (December 2001): 745–755, https://doi.org/10.1016/s0022-3999(01)00285-9.

22   Michael K. Scullin, Madison L. Krueger, Hannah K. Ballard, Natalya Pruett, and Donald L. Bliwise, "The Effects of Bedtime Writing on Difficulty Falling Asleep: A Polysomnographic Study Comparing To-Do Lists and Completed Activity Lists," *Journal of Experimental Psychology* 147, no. 1 (January 2018): 139–146, https://doi.org/10.1037/xge0000374.

23   Monika Sohal, Pavneet Singh, Bhupinder Singh Dhillon, and Harbir Singh Gill, "Efficacy of Journaling in the Management of Mental Illness: A Systematic Review and Meta-Analysis," *Family Medicine and Community Health* 10, no. 1 (March 2022), https://doi.org/10.1136/fmch-2021-001154.

24   Eric Stice, Emily Burton, Sarah Kate Bearman, Paul Rohde. "Randomized Trial of a Brief Depression Prevention Program: An Elusive Search for a Psychosocial Placebo Control Condition," *Behaviour Research and Therapy* 45, no. 5 (May 2007): 863–876, https://doi.org/10.1016/j.brat.2006.08.008.

25   Parisa Hasanzadeh, Masoud Fallahi Khoshknab, Kian Norozi, "Impacts of Journaling on Anxiety and Stress in Multiple Sclerosis Patients," *Complementary Medicine Journal* 2, no. 2 (9-2012), http://cmja.arakmu.ac.ir/browse.php.

26   Donna Bach, Gary Groesbeck, Peta Stapleton, Rebecca Sims, Katharina Blickheuser, and Dawson Church, "Clinical EFT (Emotional Freedom Techniques) Improves Multiple Physiological Markers of Health," *Journal of Evidence-Based Integrative Medicine* 24 (February 19, 2019), https://doi.org/10.1177/2515690X18823691.

27   Keith M. Diaz, Virginia J. Howard, Brent Hutto, Natalie Colabianchi, John E. Vena, Monika M. Safford, Steven N. Blair, and Steven P. Hooker, "Patterns of Sedentary Behavior and Mortality in U.S. Middle-Aged and Older Adults: A National Cohort Study," *Annals of Internal Medicine* 167, no. 7 (October 3, 2017): 465–475, https://doi.org/10.7326/M17-0212.

28   Phillip D. Tomporowski, "Effects of Acute Bouts of Exercise on Cognition," *Acta Psychologica* 112, no. 3 (March 2003): 297–324, https://doi.org/10.1016/s0001-6918(02)00134-8. Gershon Tenenbaum, Raya Uval, Gabi Elbaz, Michael Bar-Eli, and Robert Weinberg, "The Relationship Between Cognitive Characteristics and Decision Making," *Canadian Journal of Applied Physiology* 18, no. 1 (April 1993): 48–62, https://Doi.org/10.1139/h93-006.

29   Carl W. Cotman and Nicole C. Berchtold, "Exercise: A Behavioral Intervention to Enhance Brain Health and Elasticity," *Trends in Neurosciences* 25, no. 6 (June 2002): 295–301, https://doi.org/0.1016/s0166-2236(02)02143-4.

30   Neville Owen, Geneviève N. Healy, Charles E. Matthews, and David W. Dunstan, "Too Much Sitting: The Population-Health Science of Sedentary Behavior," *Exercise and Sport Science Review* 38, no. 3 (July 2010): 105–113, https://

doi.org/10.1097/JES.0b013e3181e373a2.

31   U.S. Department of Health and Human Services, *Physical Activity Guidelines for Americans*. 2nd ed. (Washington, DC: U.S. Department of Health and Human Services, 2018), https://health.gov/our-work/physical-activity/current-guidelines.

32   Dong Hoon Lee, Leandro F. M. Rezende, Hee-Kyung Joh; NaNa Keum, Gerson Ferrari; Juan Pablo Rey-Lopez; Eric B. Rimm; Fred K. Tabung; Edward L. Giovannucci, "Long-Term Leisure-Time Physical Activity Intensity and All-Cause and Cause-Specific Mortality: A Prospective Cohort of US Adults," *Circulation* 146 (July 25, 2022): 523–534. https://doi.org/10.1161/CIRCULATIONAHA.121.058162.

33   Edward R. Laskowski, "How Much Should the Average Adult Exercise Every Day?" (Mayo Clinic, September 22, 2021), https://www.mayoclinic.org/healthy-lifestyle/fitness/expert-answers/exercise/faq-20057916.

34   Edith Cowan University, "Exercise Answer: Research Shows It's How Often You Do It, Not How Much: We All Know Exercise Is Important, but Is It Better to Do a Little Every Day, or a Lot a Few Times a Week?" *ScienceDaily*, August 15, 2022.

35   Matthew N. Ahmadi, Philip J. Clare, Peter T. Katzmarzyk, Borja del Pozo Cruz, I. Min Lee, Emmanuel Stamatakis, "Vigorous Physical Activity, Incident Heart Disease, and Cancer: How Little Is Enough?" *European Heart Journal* 43, no. 46 (December 7, 2022): 4801–4814, https://doi.org/10.1093/eurheartj/ehac572.

36   Emmanuel Stamatakis, Matthew N. Ahmadi, Jason M. R. Gill, Cecilie Thogersen-Ntoumani, Martin J. Gibala, Aiden Doherty, and Mark Hamer, "Association of Wearable Device–Measured Vigorous Intermittent Lifestyle Physical Activity with Mortality," *Nature Medicine* 28 (2022): 2521–2529, https://doi.org/10.1038/s41591-022-02100-x.

37   Alan Hedge, quoted in Carina Storrs, "Stand Up, Sit Less and Move More, Researchers Say: Here's How to Do It," cnn.com, "CNN Health," (August 6, 2015), https://www.cnn.com/2015/08/06/health/how-to-move-more/index.html.

38   Maia Szalavitz, "Q&A: Jon-Kabat-Zinn Talks About Bringing Mindfulness Meditation to Medicine," *Time* (January 11, 2012), https://healthland.time.com/2012/01/11/mind-reading-jon-kabat-zinn-talks-about-bringing-mindfulness-meditation-to-medicine/.

39   *Psychology Today*, "Meditation" (*Psychology Today*, n.d.), https://www.psychologytoday.com/us/basics/meditation.

40   Simon B. Goldberg, Raymond P. Tucker, Preston A. Greene, Richard J. Davidson, Bruce E. Wampold, David J. Kearny, Tracy L. Simpson, "Mindfulness-Based Interventions for Psychiatric Disorders: A Systematic Review and Meta-Analysis," *Clinical Psychology Review* 59 (February 2018): 52–60, https://doi.org/10.1016/j.cpr.2017.10.011.

41   Burchard, *High Performance Habits*.

42   Clear, *Atomic Habits*, 70.

43   Joe Hoomans, "35,000 Decisions: The Great Choices of Strategic Leaders," *The Leading Edge* (blog), Roberts Wesleyan College, March 20, 2015, https://go.roberts.edu/leading-edge/the-great-choices-of-strategic-leaders.

44   Brian Wansink and Jeffery Sobal, "Mindless Eating: The 200 Daily Food Decisions We Overlook," *Environment and Behavior* 39, no. 1 (January 2007): 106–123, https://doi.org/10.1177/0013916506295573.

45   Clear, *Atomic Habits*, 69–72.

46   Benjamin Hardy, *Willpower Doesn't Work* (New York: Hachette, 2018), 115–116.

47   Clear, *Atomic Habits*, 33.

48   Clear, *Atomic Habits*, 38.

49   Burchard, *High Performance Habits*.

50   Clear, *Atomic Habits*, 74.

51   Hardy, *Willpower Doesn't Work*, 115–116.

52   Clear, *Atomic Habits*, 69–72.